The Cinema of Orson Welles

The Cinema of Orson Welles

PETER COWIE

"The camera is much more than a recording apparatus, it is a medium via which messages reach us from another world, a world that is not ours and that brings us to the heart of a great secret. Here magic begins . . . A film is a ribbon of dreams"—ORSON WELLES.

South Brunswick and New York: A. S. Barnes and Company
London: The Tantivy Press

© 1973 by Peter Cowie

A. S. Barnes & Co., Inc.
Cranbury, New Jersey 08512

The Tantivy Press
Magdalen House
136-148 Tooley Street
London SE1 2TT, England

FIRST PAPERBACK EDITION PUBLISHED 1978

Library of Congress Cataloging in Publication Data

Cowie, Peter.
  A ribbon of dreams.

  "Revised and enlarged version of . . . The cinema of
Orson Welles, published in 1965."
  Bibliography: p.
  1. Welles, Orson, 1915–   I. Title.
PN1998.A3W44 1972   791.43′0233′0924   79-37809
ISBN 0-498-07998-8
ISBN 0-498-02298-6 (paperback)

Originally published as A RIBBON OF DREAMS: The Cinema of Orson Welles

Printed in the United States of America

This book is for Mutti

Contents

Author's Note

THE SMALL NUMBERS SCATTERED throughout the text refer the reader to the Bibliography in Appendix 5. Each item in this list of sources is numbered, and those numbers in the text correspond to the entries in the Bibliography.

Quotations marked with an asterisk in the text are drawn from a personal interview between Mr. Welles and the author in 1963; those marked with a dagger are extracted from a letter from Mr. Welles to the author.

The script extracts from *Citizen Kane* originally appeared in the French magazine *L'Avant-Scène du Cinéma*, Number 11, January 1962. The author is most grateful to this journal for permission to reprint the extracts, which he has revised according to the English version of the film (and not according to the continuity published in Pauline Kael's *The Citizen Kane Book*, which deviates in points of detail from the actual film).

Finally, the author wishes to express his appreciation of Mr. Welles's help during the original preparation of this work.

> *Note:* this volume is a much revised and enlarged version of the author's paperback book, *The Cinema of Orson Welles*, published in 1965.

Acknowledgements

THE AUTHOR AND PUBLISHERS wish to thank the following for their help in providing illustrations and other material for this book: ABC TV (London), L'Avant-Scène, John Baxter, Robin Bean, BBC, British Lion, Ivan Butler, Columbia Pictures, Contemporary Films, Raymond Durgnat, Don Fredericksen, Janus Films, Jugoslavija Film, Joseph McBride, David Meeker, Mary Morris, M-G-M, National Film Archive, Barrie Pattison, Planet Films, Rank Organisation, Republic, RKO, Anne Rogers, Nicolas Tikhomiroff/Uniphoto, Twentieth Century-Fox, Universal-International, Information Department of the British Film Institute (Brenda Davies, Peter Seward, Gillian Hartnoll), and especially Fred Zentner and his Cinema Bookshop.

Introduction

"A film is never really good
unless the camera is an eye
in the head of a poet"—
ORSON WELLES[10]

MOST WRITERS ABOUT FILM pass swiftly through two phases.
There is the first, rapturous discovery of film technique—deep-focus
photography, crane shots, long takes, the sheer sculptured beauty of
Last Year in Marienbad or *The Eclipse,* the sensual satisfaction of the
colour in *Klute* or *Claire's Knee.* Then comes a suspicious reaction
against flamboyance for its own sake, and a concentration on subject
and theme (not "content," which can, arguably, be regarded as style
in itself); on the film in which—with a strictly self-effacing skill—a
director deals with human dilemmas. Honesty rather than panache
becomes the critic's criterion.

But beyond these two phases lies an awareness that the true creators
are those whose work could not be fashioned or expressed in any but
cinematic terms—the film-makers whose obsession with the cinema
and its magical, illusionist properties is in intimate harmony with their
own vision of life. Thus such apparently diverse figures as Stroheim,
Bergman, Buñuel, Ford, Renoir, Resnais, Welles, and Satyajit Ray
loom as indisputable masters. In his first phase, a critic may exult in
Bergman, Resnais, and Welles; in his second phase he may admire
Ford, Renoir, and Buñuel. And then he will surely sense that they
all belong to what *Cahiers du Cinéma* term loftily the "Pantheon"
(alongside, of course, the Marx Brothers, whose anarchic refusal to be
bounded by the conventions of vaudeville is as great a homage to the
cinema's powers of enchantment as any movie by Lang or Kubrick).

On viewing Welles's work yet again for the purpose of revising and
expanding the little paperback on his films that I wrote seven years
ago, I am more than ever convinced of his place among the immortals.
Here is an artist whose humanism and ideas have triumphed over the
flashy, meretricious image that critics from Kerr to Kael have imposed
on him. It is the mature passion of Welles's cinema that counts; a

13

cinema in which romance and dreams still hold sway at a time when bitter realism is the arbiter of taste. Suddenly the frantic haste of Arkadin's methods in *Confidential Report* and the slow solemnity of Clay's in *The Immortal Story,* the writhing jealousy of Othello and the sad jests of Falstaff, the Irish blarney of Michael O'Hara in *The Lady from Shanghai* and the capricious scheming of Georgie Minafer in *The Magnificent Ambersons*—suddenly these things are meaningful solely because of the way in which Welles has conceived them and registered them on his ribbon of celluloid, his "ribbon of dreams," and for that we must all, in the end, be grateful.

★　　★　　★

"Let us drink," says Arkadin, "to those who, as Shakespeare had it, can to themselves be true . . . no matter what their nature may be." The most consistent aspect of the career of Orson Welles is this truthfulness of which Arkadin speaks. Welles has always responded to his nature as an artist of enormously varied talents. It has not been easy, in the face of the hostility and distrust of Hollywood and, in the Fifties and Sixties, of an ungrateful English-speaking press. As he wrote to the *New Statesman* in 1958: "I've been given the use of my tools exactly eight times in twenty years. Just once my own editing of the film has been the version put into release; and (excepting the Shakespearian experiments) I have only twice been given any voice at all as to the 'level' of my subject matter."[12] The special Academy Award bestowed on him in 1971 was, one felt, an instinctive attempt by the film colony to atone for its attitude to Welles.

But Welles the film-maker, with whom I am concerned in this book, is only a part of Welles the man. Born on May 6, 1915, at Kenosha, Wisconsin, he was the son of Richard Head Welles, an industrialist, and Beatrice Ives Welles. His mother was, among other things, a concert pianist, an ardent suffragette and a respectable rifle shot. Ravel and Stravinsky were friends of hers. Welles quickly attracted attention throughout the United States as a "child wonder." His precocity was such that he could read fluently at two, and at seven he was able to recite by heart any speech from *King Lear.* He adapted Shakespearian plays and wrote plays of his own long before he was ten. "I was a *Wunderkind* of music. I played the violin, piano, I conducted. My mother died when I was nine, and I never played again—it was a kind of trauma."[26] Welles's passions still include painting and magic. During his life he has written novels and has been responsible for some memorable stage productions. His abilities as an actor are considerable and

Welles enjoys his magic with Joseph Cotten and Dolores Costello.

are discussed in a separate chapter. He is an ardent follower of bull-
fighting and has acted as a *picador* in Seville.

Unlike so many infant prodigies, Welles continued to shock the
world well into his twenties. At sixteen he was in Ireland, convincing
Hilton Edwards and Micheál MacLiammóir at the Gate Theatre,
Dublin, that he was a leading star of the New York Theater Guild,
and striking up thereby a friendship that was to result in—apart from
stage productions—*Othello* and *Return to Glennascaul*.

In 1934 he shot a four minute filmlet entitled *The Hearts of Age*,
featuring himself and his first wife Virginia Nicholson. Co-directed
with William Vance and made during a drama festival at his own old
school in Woodstock, Illinois, *The Hearts of Age* has been seen by
few critics. Joseph McBride terms it "an allegory of death," with Welles
himself "mincing and leering, in a sort of comic Irishman costume,
his face grotesquely aged like the lady's, his hairline masked and a
wispy clown wig protruding from the temples."[108] There are negative

effects, inserts, and tilted shots, with Virginia Nicholson as an old lady *and* a Keystone Kop, and Vance as an Indian swathed in a blanket.

By 1937 Welles had founded the Mercury Theatre, which beside yielding players like Joseph Cotten and Everett Sloane to the cinema via *Citizen Kane,* provoked widespread interest because of the unusual flavour of its productions (among them *Faust* and a modern dress version of *Julius Caesar*). Welles alternated radio with his theatrical work, and in 1938 he became notorious overnight when thousands of Americans took his presentation of H. G. Wells's *The War of the Worlds* as a genuine reportage (it was scripted by Howard Koch). Shortly afterwards this paragon of the arts was approached by RKO with a view to his making a film, and probably a series of films, for them in Hollywood. The ensuing contract gave Welles an unprecedented control over the film as well as twenty-five percent of its gross receipts and an advance of 150,000 dollars on the contract. It's difficult to tell if the RKO producers had seen *Too Much Johnson,* the name given to a half hour film made in 1938 by Welles and his team (including John Houseman and Richard Wilson) specifically to accompany—as prologue and interlude—a stage production of the William Gillette comedy melodrama about a rake (played by Joseph Cotten) pursued by the outraged husband of his French mistress. According to Charles Higham, "Rooftops were used for chases, in the style of the Keystone Kops with Joseph Cotten frequently risking his life as he hung from rooftops, Harold Lloyd style. A Bronx studio was used for the interiors."[47] Welles also shot a film to introduce *The Green Goddess,* a vaudeville show he staged in 1939. This, his associate Richard Wilson is reported as saying, depicted an air crash in the Himalayas.

Although *Citizen Kane* appeared in the form he desired, Welles's teething pains in the cinema industry began in 1939 when his plans for shooting adaptations of Joseph Conrad's *Heart of Darkness* (in which he would have played Marlow and Kurtz, the two key characters) and Nicholas Blake's *The Smiler with the Knife* (with Carole Lombard, Lucille Ball, or Rosalind Russell) were abandoned. And after the *furore* over *Citizen Kane,* RKO began drawing in their horns. *The Magnificent Ambersons* was edited behind Welles's back and he was recalled from South America in the midst of shooting *It's All True.* His contract was at an end. Henceforth Welles was *persona non grata* with the big studios, although he was to make three more films before withdrawing to Europe.

For more than twenty years he has wandered around Europe, acting in other people's productions in ceaseless efforts to finance the torrent of films that fill his imagination. *The Odyssey, The Iliad, War and*

Welles with Jeanne Moreau in THE SAILOR FROM GIBRALTAR.

Welles shares a joke with an ABC TV interview team in London.

Peace, Noah, Salome, and *The Pickwick Papers* have all been visualized cinematically in his mind, but have never been brought to the screen for lack of funds. He has made a film in a few days (*Macbeth*), and a film over a period of years (*Don Quixote*). But in spite of the obstacles he seems forever confronted with, Welles readily agrees that "the greatest danger for an artist is to find himself in a comfortable position."[51] With the typical modesty to which anyone who has talked with him will testify, he has also said: "I do not suppose I shall be remembered for anything. But I don't think about my work in those terms. It is just as vulgar to work for the sake of posterity as to work for the sake of money."[25]

★   ★   ★

Before discussing *Citizen Kane* in detail, it may be useful to try and set Welles's achievement in perspective. Everyone is agreed that the film fell like a bomb on established Hollywood conventions (rather too many of which survived the blast). But Welles did not *invent* any new cinematic processes: he fused the experience of three decades into one gigantic work that proclaimed with tremendous power just how effective a medium the cinema could be. He assimilated the styles and subtleties the cinema had evolved, often unwittingly, since Griffith. For practically every technical device in *Citizen Kane* there is a precedent; but there is no precedent for *Citizen Kane,* the film.

Much as Truffaut has wanted to follow in the steps of Hitchcock, so Welles, one feels, has sought affinities with John Ford. And while Truffaut is in practice closer to Renoir than he is to Hitchcock, Welles's vision is expressed not so much in Fordian terms as in the style of the German directors of the Twenties. The relaxed *bonhomie* of Ford's world eludes him, except in parts of *The Stranger* and *Chimes at Midnight.* But Welles uses architecture with much the same strength as Reinhardt's pupils did (Welles admits that German and Russian theatre influenced him early on, even though he had not seen any German movies). The castle wreathed with clouds at the start of *Citizen Kane* and *Macbeth* is remote, haunting, and Wagnerian in its suggestion of power. Arkadin's turreted headquarters in Spain, the clock tower that looms over *The Stranger,* or the Gothic mass of Henry IV's Windsor in *Chimes at Midnight,* are metaphors for vaulting oppression, all viewed from low camera set-ups to emphasise their physical weight.

The geometric groupings in *Macbeth* recall Fritz Lang's *Siegfried,* the psychological force of staircases in *The Magnificent Ambersons* and *Othello* recall such German classics as *Asphalt, Hintertreppe,* and *Pandora's Box.* Welles's recurrent use of mirrors brings to mind *The Last Laugh* or *Berlin, Rhythm of a City.* His rendering of what the Germans call *Stimmung* (mood) is controlled by means of light and mist, as in *Der mude Tod,* as well as through superimpositions (several images from *Ambersons* and *The Lady from Shanghai* have their counterparts in *Secrets of a Soul*). The vast gatherings of people in *The Trial,* in and outside the court, or at K's office, remind one of *Metropolis* with its cowed workers, blindly subservient to an almost abstract power. And the central battle for supremacy in Welles's world is waged between darkness and light, producing a wealth of chiaroscuro effects that could be those of Pabst, Lang, or Dupont. Like these German masters, Welles regards power with an unmistakable foreboding. It is built up, only to be destroyed. Destiny waits in the wings of Welles's stage, as inexorable a presence as it is in the German tradition. And the guilt that marks *The Stranger* is echoed in Peter Lorre's *Der Verlorene* (1950), with its grey, fearful imagery and its central protagonist almost dragged to crime by his own complexes.

During the Thirties, Hollywood had consolidated its influence over the cinema. Hundreds of films poured from its studios each year. Yet *Citizen Kane* marked much more than the bright spark of a new decade, and it is tempting and justifiable to divide cinema history into the pre-1940 and post-1940 periods. The gangster films, comedies and Westerns of the Thirties had all established an elaborate iconography of their own. But dialogue and situation took precedence over style and expression. The American cinema prior to *Kane* was undoubtedly one of illusion—and the cinema of Welles is one of illusion dispelled.

Welles, the amateur *in excelsis,* brought the experiment of youth to an industry where most directors were middle-aged professionals— Capra, Ford, Hawks, Milestone, Wellman, Curtiz, Vidor, LeRoy etc. He also proved, with his enviable contract, that a director in Hollywood could enjoy as much artistic freedom as Sjöström and Stiller had in Sweden or Lang and Murnau in Germany during the silent period. Only Sternberg before him had managed to exert such comprehensive control over his material in America, and even he had fallen foul of Paramount over *Blonde Venus.*

Economically, too, the West Coast studios were at a crucial stage in their life. The Second World War reduced Hollywood's overseas market at a stroke and, though they barely knew it, the major companies were never again to assert quite the same measure of dominance they had in the high Thirties. Independent producers became the great white hopes of the industry. Welles, who was on good terms with Jack Warner, Harry Cohn, Darryl Zanuck and other studio heads, says that, "the minute the independents got in, I never directed another American picture except by accident. . . . I was a maverick, but the studios understood what that meant, and if there was a fight, we both enjoyed it."[36]

Deep-focus photography had been employed before, as will be shown in the following chapter; but Welles turned to this process not so much to show his ability to solve a technical problem as to help in the evolution of a highly personal and articulate style. As André Bazin commented, ". . . artistic invention in Welles is always subordinated to the pursuit of an intimate expression, to the creation of characters, to a vision of the world."[41]

This vision of the world is one of the most controversial features of Welles's work in the cinema. One either loves or hates his characters. At best they are like the figures of Dostoievsky, demented and impelled by some hidden Protean force; at worst they are like many Dickensian characters, thrust in briefly, overdrawn to the point of farce, pathetic in their contortions and glib statements. Yet all of them are eminently human. Nearly all of them are endowed with humorous qualities that lighten for an instant their brooding, menacing surroundings. Welles's world is divided into predators and victims or, to use Arkadin's metaphor, into scorpions and frogs. People of the order of Kane, Georgie Minafer, Iago, Quinlan, Elsa Bannister, Hastler, and Prince Hal, prey on those who stand for reasonable behaviour, like Leland, Eugene Morgan, O'Hara, Othello, Vargas, Joseph K and Falstaff. None of these characters obeys a moral code. They are not, like the helpless heroes of Bergman's later period, confounded by any deep-rooted ethic. They hammer out among themselves a rough code of justice: he that resorts to violence shall perish violently. They all regard themselves as above the law and Quinlan, in his abuse of police power, is no different to Kane in his abuse of the press and the liberty of expression. They are wanderers—even the "frogs" like O'Hara and Van Stratten—in search of their own identity and are obsessed by this task even if, as in the case of Kane, it is done for them by someone else.

The leading figures in Welles's films are brought to their knees by a single fatal flaw, as in classical or Shakespearian tragedy; they are nearly all Manichean, unscrupulous, and damned; yet they are all capable of arousing one's sympathies. Welles has expressed it thus: "I don't detest them, I detest the way they act—that is my point of tension. All the characters I've played are various forms of Faust. I hate all forms of Faust, because I believe it's impossible for Man to be great without admitting there is something greater than himself—either the law of God or art—but there must be something greater than Man. I have sympathy for those characters—humanly, but not morally."[43] Welles's playing in these parts is usually excellent and enables one to differentiate between the man's passion, which can be condemned, and the man himself, who may be excused.

Thus, throughout Welles's *oeuvre,* there is a marked absence of colourless figures. He is never one for half measures, an attitude reflected in his remark: "I have a great love and respect for religion, great love and respect for atheism. What I hate is agnosticism, people who do not choose."[27] Equally, no action is left incomplete, no spring of tragedy unwound. Power is established only to be destroyed; the more massive the power, the more reverberating its fall. The poignancy of the situation is heightened because these characters always realise their plight in a moment of agonising and unexpected truth in the film —when Quinlan talks finally to Tanya, when Major Amberson speaks after Isabel's death, when Arkadin bellows in impotent rage for a seat on the plane that is bearing Van Stratten away to his beloved daughter. The act of destruction is repeatedly symbolised in an image of the Fall:

the fall of Elsa and Arthur Bannister among the mirrors, the fall of Arkadin's plane, the fall of Quinlan into the filthy river, the fall of Franz Kindler from the clock tower, the fall of the shell from Clay's lifeless fingers. Death is everywhere in Welles's films, sometimes at the outset (the death-throes of Kane, the suicide of Arkadin, the funeral rites of Othello, the successful assassination of Linnekar on the Mexican border) and sometimes at the end, "all passion spent" (Macbeth, Quinlan, Joseph K, the Bannisters, Falstaff, Clay).

The heroes of Welles's world are human in several respects, as one has seen, but one of the principles that seems to underlie these films is that material ambition will always override human relationships. The most straightforward example is Macbeth, but the careers of Kane, Quinlan, Arkadin, and the Bannisters offer equally valid evidence of this. When Kane tells his wife at the breakfast table that her only rival is the *Inquirer*, she muses: "Sometimes I think I'd prefer a rival of flesh and blood." In *The Magnificent Ambersons*, Georgie Minafer frustrates the marriage of Isabel and Eugene; in *Touch of Evil* Quinlan's only friend, Menzies, eventually revolts against him. Perhaps the most embittered ending to a love affair in Welles's work is when Elsa, in *The Lady from Shanghai*, is abandoned by Michael O'Hara and sobs out after him, "Give my love to the sunrise!" This sentence is as revealing a comment as any on the blighted aims and lives of so many Wellesian protagonists.

The Cinema of Orson Welles

The Films

"I don't love films. I love making films"
ORSON WELLES[31]

CITIZEN KANE

"We can get Kane out of our minds, but not Kane's dream"
—WILLIAM WHITEBAIT

PLOT OUTLINE—Charles Foster Kane dies at the age of seventy-six in his immense castle, Xanadu; his dying word is "Rosebud." In the projection room of a newsreel firm, a group of reporters notes that Kane's public life—wealth, political and social events—does not contain the answer to the enigmatic "Rosebud." A reporter, Thompson, sets out to find the solution and, after reading the details of Kane's ruptured childhood, interviews four leading figures in the magnate's life: Bernstein, Leland (both associates of Kane at the height of his career) ; his second wife, Susan Alexander, whom Kane had forced to become an opera singer against her will and who is now drunk in a dingy night club; and Raymond, Kane's butler in the concluding stages of his life at Xanadu. All these people are most forthcoming. Some even give different versions of the same events. But none can explain to Thompson the implications of the word "Rosebud." The answer is given to the audience at the end: as Kane's belongings are packed up and removed from Xanadu, a workman tosses an old sledge into a fire. Painted on it is the word "Rosebud." It is the dim memory of his childhood toy that has haunted Kane throughout his life and on his deathbed.

CITIZEN KANE was made in the late summer and early autumn of 1940, and it took Welles several months, working six days a week, to edit. "I've worked hard since I came to Hollywood—very hard on the shooting of *Citizen Kane* (normal hours 4 A.M. to 10 P.M.) ."[89] Earlier, Welles had studied the more important films in the Museum of Modern Art. "John Ford was my teacher. My own style has nothing

27

Welles as Kane, young, brash, successful.

to do with his, but *Stagecoach* was my movie text-book. I ran it over forty times."[34] Then, just prior to shooting the film, he spent several weeks on the sets, making himself familiar with the routine and the equipment. He refused to listen to technicians who told him that what he wanted to do was impossible. Shooting finally began on July 30, one year precisely after Welles had arrived in the film colony. "Quite simply, I was left alone. Like a painter's or a writer's, my work was my own and nobody else's, to be respected as private property, not handed over for processing on the assembly line. That freedom has never again been entrusted to me."[21]

Almost more space has been devoted by critics to the outcry caused by *Citizen Kane* at the time of its opening than to its cinematic merits. However, a short account of events may help to place the film in its historical context. The trouble began when word reached William Randolph Hearst that Welles's film was a caricature of his life. Hearst was a newspaper tycoon like Kane, and the resemblance between the two men seemed to extend even to small details, including lines of dialogue characteristic of Hearst. Susan Alexander was immediately said to correspond to Marion Davies, the starlet with whom Hearst had fallen in love in 1918, only two years after Kane had supposedly met Susan (both women were addicted to jigsaws!). Louis B. Mayer, via Nicholas Schenck, offered RKO the $842,000 the film had cost to make if only they would burn it before it was released, so fearful was the industry of reprisals by the Hearst empire. When this move failed, Hearst threatened to attack the entire American film world in his press. RKO encountered difficulty in obtaining circuit bookings for the film, because Warners, Loews, and Paramount all relied heavily on the Hearst papers for advertising outlets. Eventually RKO exhibited *Citizen Kane* solely in their own cinemas, and in New York and Los Angeles independent halls had to be hired. Hearst, as a result, banned his papers from mentioning any RKO films. The scheduled opening was originally February 14, 1941, but the violent clash between Hearst and the production company delayed the first public screening until May 1, 1941, in New York (although the press saw the film privately during March—"Few movies have ever come from Hollywood with such forceful narrative, such original technique, such exciting photography," raved *Life*). To this day, Welles studiously denies that he and Mankiewicz modelled Kane on Hearst ("Kane would have liked to see a film of his life," he told me, "but not Hearst—he didn't have quite enough style."*).

Citizen Kane is above all the study of a personality. It is not, as critics have often been led to assert, a frontal attack on the monopolies of American big business and politics (as is, say, Robert Rossen's *All the King's Men* or Elia Kazan's *A Face in the Crowd*); nor is it the study of a man's mind and private preoccupations (as is, say, Ingmar Bergman's *Wild Strawberries*). Kane remains a personality whose eminence and publicity depend solely on his ability to project his own magniloquent image; he becomes a symbol ("Few private lives were more public," booms the newsreel). The fact that he is a press magnate helps to counterpoint the excessive publicity he achieves, but is no more vital to the theme than "Rosebud" itself. His life and influence are seen not through his own eyes, but through those of other people. The entire film is a major reportage (without using that term in its pejorative sense), an enlargement and extension of the newsreel at the beginning. "This might be called a 3-D film, with time instead of spatial depth as the salient third dimension," claims William Johnson.[92] Thus the flashback method employed by Welles and Mankiewicz is essential to the success of the film. "The truth about Kane," wrote Welles at the time of the film's release, "like the truth about any man, can only be calculated by the sum of everything that has been said about him."[89]

Welles has never denied the contribution of Mankiewicz to the script, neither on the credits of *Kane* (when countless other Hollywood screenwriters were often ignored on the finished print of productions they had helped to create), nor in later interviews. "He wrote several important scenes," he said in 1965. "I was very lucky to work with Mankiewicz: everything concerning Rosebud belongs to him."[29] To say that Mankiewicz created the script of *Kane* as it appears on the screen is to imply that all Welles's subsequent work is a pastiche of Mankiewicz's style and dialogue. Pauline Kael's lengthy but scrappy investigation of the movie's birth pangs proves chapter and verse that Kane *was* Hearst, with knobs on. But her championship of Mankiewicz's script (written in early 1940 while Welles was taping weekly radio shows with the Mercury team in Hollywood and also working on *his Kane* script) still leaves one certain of Welles's guiding hand and flashes of inspiration to guide the operation along.

Mankiewicz's major contribution was probably the "prismatic" idea —a man's life viewed from several angles, which has not recurred in any other Welles film, and the "force of journalism" that Miss Kael finds so praiseworthy. According to Mankiewicz's secretary, Mrs.

Kane drafts his "Declaration of Principles," as Leland (Joseph Cotten) and Bernstein (Everett Sloane) look on.

Alexander (whose name he took for Susan in the film) , "Welles didn't write (or dictate) one line of the shooting script of *Citizen Kane.*"[48] But, as Welles wrote to the London *Times* on November 17, 1971, Herman Mankiewicz "denounced it [the final version of the screenplay] roundly on the basis of 'rushes' which he saw at various times after our filming had begun. His indignation certainly came largely from the fact that the actual shooting script differed so drastically from his own work and had, in fact, been completed in the absence of any consultations with himself or Mr. John Houseman."[13] Besides, the scene in the *Inquirer* office when Welles finishes Leland's review for him must surely have its origins if not its precise dialogue in the incident in Welles's fifteenth year when he was a ghost writer for a music critic. "He was too drunk to write his copy. The widow is still alive, so I can't tell you his name."[39]

All this is not to denigrate the memory of Herman Mankiewicz who, indeed, had forty-six credits to his name before *Citizen Kane.* It merely seems rather pompous to pretend that a masterpiece like *Kane* owes its greatness to a co-scriptwriter; just as ludicrous as it would be

to pretend that Joseph Stefano (or Robert Bloch) was responsible
for the stature of *Psycho,* or Ulla Isaksson for anything other than the
bare quality of *The Virgin Spring.*

★ ★ ★

Kane is all things to all men. To Welles himself, "Kane is a man
who abuses the power of the popular press and also sets himself up
against the law, against the entire tradition of liberal civilisation,"[25]
and "at once egotistical and disinterested . . . at once an idealist and a
swindler, a very great man and a mediocre individual."[42] To Thatcher,
his erstwhile guardian, in his statement to the press, he is "nothing
more or less—a Communist," a ruthless egotist who does not know
how to handle money; rather more than a spoilt child. To the newsreel
compilers and to "forty-four million news readers," he is a colossal,
larger-than-life tycoon who dominated four decades of American life.
To Susan, his mistress and subsequent wife, he appears as an awesome
monster who launched her on her disastrous career as a singer without

*Kane cheerfully faces the fact of a small circulation, with Leland and
Bernstein.*

even asking her permission; mean, materialistic, and incapable of loving anyone. To Leland, his college friend, he is cynical and faintly malevolent ("He never gave himself away, he never gave anything away, he just left you a tip") and "always trying to prove something." To Bernstein, his General Manager, he was perhaps most congenial, "a man who lost almost everything he had," a man to be pitied and revered. (It is interesting to note, by the way, that Welles's own mentor in youth was a certain Doctor Bernstein who presented him, among other things, with a puppet theatre when he was in his infancy.) To Thompson, the reporter, "Mr. Kane was a man who got everything he wanted and then lost it."

To Raymond, his calculating *major domo* at Xanadu, Kane is a pathetic old fool. To himself, Kane is quite simply a wholly autonomous man. "There's only one person in this world who decides what I'm going to do, and that's me," he tells Emily in the scene with Gettys in Susan's rooms. When his newspapers are hit by the 1929 depression he says to Thatcher and Bernstein, "Well, I always gagged on that silver spoon. You know, Mr. Bernstein, if I hadn't been very rich, I might have been a really great man." Yet with the years this honesty of appraisal gradually vanishes; Kane behaves as if money were capable of purchasing everything in life, even simple abstract commodities like greatness. He weaves about himself a myth that ultimately even he acknowledges to be the truth; his fleeting references to "Rosebud" always emanate from his subconscious and so he can never grasp the exact nature of the lacuna that has prevented him from plotting an entirely satisfactory life. As André Bazin observed in this context, it is worth nothing to conquer the world if one has lost one's childhood.[41]

As if to compensate for the loss of his beloved sledge, Kane devotes a large part of his life to the acquisition of material objects. He garners them omnivorously, from the world's biggest diamond ("I didn't know Charlie was collecting diamonds," says Leland; "He ain't," replies Bernstein, "He's collecting somebody that's collecting diamonds") to "the biggest private zoo since Noah." And all that he achieves through these possessions are manifold reflections of his own ego, symbolized in the mirror Kane limps past at Xanadu near the end. The statues and other artistic bric-à-brac of Xanadu suggest Kane's futile inability to *create*. Nothing remains after his death, except the black smoke that wells into the air from the chimneys of his palace, as his "junk," the sledge among it, is consigned to the flames. Of the people who linger within his power, Bernstein alone remains a faithful apostle. Leland denies him, as Peter denied Christ. Bazin maintains

The first clue to "Rosebud." Thatcher (George Coulouris) greets his charge (Buddy Swan), while father (Harry Shannon) and mother (Agnes Moorehead) look on.

that Kane is at last avenged on his parents and on Thatcher "by playing with his social power like a huge toboggan, so as to thrill himself with the dizziness of fortune, or by hitting those who dare to cast aspersion on the moral basis of his actions and his pleasure."[41]

The problem of "Rosebud" deserves some attention. Welles himself is the first to admit that, "It's a gimmick, really, and rather dollar-book Freud."[34] And as Thompson says resignedly at the close of the film, "I don't think any word can explain a man's life. No, I guess 'Rosebud' is just a piece in a jigsaw puzzle—a missing piece." The sledge is not so precious in itself to Kane (one never sees him look at it, even though it lies amid his belongings at Xanadu) but it conjures up for him memories of a childhood innocence far removed from the "Chicago, New York, and Washington" to which he was so brusquely introduced by Thatcher. The scene in the paperweight that he finds in Susan's room in Xanadu and keeps close to him until his death is of a cottage in a snowstorm, strikingly similar to the lodging house of Mrs. Kane. "The three clues to 'Rosebud' appear at times when Kane is being treated most remotely—in the cryptic death scene in the beginning, in the unfriendly memoirs of his banker guardian, and in the final flashback narration of a cynical butler. The narrations of his closest acquaintances yield no clues to the symbolic truth of his life."[121] Welles's most overt emphasis on the sentimental importance of "Rosebud" is in his three lap-dissolves, showing the abandoned sledge being gradually covered by a snowfall after the young Kane has left with Mr. Thatcher, with the final dissolve revealing Charles beside his guardian's Christmas tree, fingering a replacement sledge with patent dissatisfaction. Just how the sledge eventually reached Xanadu is not explained, although one may conjecture from Kane's first conversation with Susan Alexander that he brought it with his mother's belongings to a warehouse in west Manhattan ("in search of my youth," he tells Susan).

Bernstein comes close to the feeling, if not the fact, behind "Rosebud" when he evokes for Thompson an occasion on the New Jersey ferry in 1896 when he had glimpsed a girl in a white dress with a white parasol. "I only saw her for one second. She didn't see me at all, but I'll bet a month hasn't gone by since that I haven't thought of that girl." Thus, because "Rosebud" does *not,* as one would expect, turn out to be the name of a girl, it stands as a token of Kane's unhappy relations with people in general. He has no friends, only acquaintances, for he insists on setting himself on a pedestal above those who seek to know him. Arrogance and lack of moral respect are the vices that lead to his isolation. Thompson, in his second interview with Susan in Atlantic City, observes: "All the same, you know, I can't help being a little sorry for Mr. Kane," to which Susan replies without a moment's hesitation, "Don't you think I do?" It is of course partly due to Welles's own sympathetic performance that one feels a measure of pity for this magnate who strives so hard to overcome his fundamental lack of spiritual fibre.

Is there, in effect, a sound case to be argued for Kane? Susan's charge—that he made her into an opera singer against her will—is quite clearly unfair, especially as in her first meeting with him she admits that she has always longed to be a singer (although this is recalled by Leland, and is therefore suspect because presumably Leland heard only Kane's version of that encounter). Leland himself, though outwardly an endearing personality, is surely ungrateful to Kane when one considers Bernstein's remark that he was the son of a man whose debts at his death were immense. Even Leland admits with sarcasm, "Maybe Charlie wasn't a brutal man—maybe he just did brutal things." Raymond, with his transparent lust for money (he asks Thompson for a thousand dollars in exchange for information about "Rosebud") is quickly shown to be no more than a parasite on the aging Kane. And Thatcher's testament is of purely biographical interest, its irascible attacks on his *protégé* consisting of part jealousy, part disgust, and part hypocrisy. When all is considered, the two unforgivable sins (in the eyes of the world) committed by Charles Foster Kane are his neglect of the perfectly harmless Emily, his first wife, and his overriding egotism, which ruins the lives of so many, even if some of them almost ask to be manoeuvred by his fancy. His insatiable desire for material wealth also condemns him in the opinion of society; but the point to be stressed here is that Kane at least gave his money back to the community, spent it moreover on works of art that endure in fossilised solitude rather than on sensual pleasures: indeed, the actual comforts

Kane and Bernstein joke at the expense of the blundering Mr. Carter (Erskine Sanford).

of Xanadu seem Spartan in the extreme, and the massive picnic at the end strikes one as inappropriate for this reason. Despite inheriting on trust the "world's sixth largest private fortune," Kane firmly rejected the easy life. He was never one to live on his interest.

So *Citizen Kane* is ruled by two mutually opposed strains: Kane's megalomania drives him forward to new experiences, triumphs, and disasters; while an intimate longing for what Welles might term the "lost paradise" of his childhood applies a brake to his headlong progress.

★   ★   ★

Kane's quest for love is the theme that prevents the film from settling into a rigid, inhuman mould. As Leland tells Thompson so glibly, "He married for love. Love. That's why he did everything. That's why he went into politics. Seems we weren't enough, he wanted all the voters to love him too. Guess all he wanted out of life was love; that's Charlie's story, how he lost it. Y'see, he just didn't have any to give. Oh, he loved Charlie Kane of course—very dearly. And his mother, I guess he always loved her." In the wake of the election defeat, Leland sneers at Kane, "You want love on your own terms, something to be played according to your rules." Shortly afterwards, Kane lifts his glass to Leland's with an ironic toast. "To love, on my terms. Those are the only terms anybody ever knows—his own." When Leland tears up the $25,000 severance cheque Kane sends him, one feels a twinge of compassion for the giver; Kane is continually finding that money cannot buy the kind of affection he craves. In the picnic tent in the Everglades, Susan accuses him: "You never really gave me anything that belongs to you, that you care about . . . You never gave me anything in your whole life, you just tried to buy me into getting you something."

Critics have dismissed as implausible the sudden yearning Kane has for Susan Alexander's company. But the dialogue, Welles's acting, and his direction of Dorothy Comingore, all combine to reveal the source of Kane's infatuation. "I don't know many people," she says. "I know too *many* people," he replies. "I guess we're both lonely." Susan, with her simplicity, her lack of sophistication, and her breathless charm, is in utter contrast to the people with whom Kane has spent his adult life. He sees her as someone in whose vacant personality he can shelter, someone through whom he can project his artistic pretensions and bask in the reflected glory. The relevance of this scene to Kane's childhood security is discreetly indicated by the presence of

*Still young and happy: above, Kane shyly announces his engagement;
below, wedding with the President's niece on the White House lawn.*

Kane, splashed with mud, makes the acquaintance of Susan Alexander (Dorothy Comingore).

the paperweight on Susan's dressing table. Furthermore, by helping Susan, Kane feels that he may be able in some obscure way to repay the debt he owes to his mother.

There is a subtle musical reminder of this theme. Hermann's boisterous "What is his name, what is his name?" song tune from the *Inquirer* party sequence is repeated at the political rally just after Kane threatens to indict, prosecute, and convict Boss Jim W. Gettys. Then it returns, plaintively on an accordion, to the background after the election disaster, as a crestfallen Kane says goodnight to Bernstein in the newspaper offices. Finally, the melody is there on the soundtrack behind the credits. It is one of those tunes that, when played or sung vigorously, has a youthful, innocent ring; and when played slowly and with restraint, it is like an echo of strayed romance. For Herrmann, who had never before scored a picture, *Citizen Kane* was an exhilarating experience. "I worked on the film, reel by reel, as it was being shot and cut. In this way I had a sense of the picture being built, and of my own music being a part of that building."[89]

★ ★ ★

Susan plays and sings while Kane enjoys the atmosphere of her room.

Citizen Kane is of primary importance in the history of the cinema because of the audacity and virtuosity of Welles's technique, and because of the influence that the style was to exert on films in all parts of the world for the next two decades. It can now be regarded as being a clear fifteen years ahead of its time, and even then it does not fit into any orthodox pattern of aesthetic progress. It remains, like some of Welles's other work, a creation fantastic and unique, a breathtaking reflection of the genius of its inventor (*pace* Pauline Kael). Critics have tried to pin down its significance by drawing literary and dramatic parallels: "For the first time on the screen we have seen the equivalent of a novel by Dos Passos,"[41] and "Apart from its cinematic importance, *Citizen Kane* constitutes, from the point of view of construction, a revolution such as dramatic art has scarcely undergone since Aeschylus"[66]; and, more lucid, Dilys Powell's review when the film first came to England in 1941: "There is no question here of experiment for experiment's sake; it is a question of a man with a problem of narrative to solve, using lighting, setting, sound, camera angles and movement much as a genuine writer uses words, phrases, cadences, rhythms; using them with the ease and boldness and resource of one who controls and is not controlled by his medium."

Yet many of the technical devices used so successfully by Welles

Kane in age, outside the opera house.

had been introduced prior to 1940. His brilliance stems from his ability to synthesise and harmonise all possible stylistic methods into a coherent instrument for telling his story. Only Gregg Toland, the lighting cameraman, agreed with Welles in adopting deep-focus photography and covered sets, and was rewarded with a credit equal in size to that of the director himself on the finished film. Toland was born in Illinois in 1904, worked a great deal with Wyler and, on his death in 1948, was the highest-paid cameraman in Hollywood. "There's never been anyone else in his class," says Welles.*

Each scene in *Citizen Kane* was provided with a ceiling, not partial (as had often been done before) but complete. "I suppose that closing the top of a set was the real revolution we caused. It's disastrous to let a cameraman light a set without a ceiling—it's artificial."* Toland was able to use the "pan-focus" process he had developed for two years. It allowed the camera to record objects at a range of a couple of feet or seventy yards with equal clarity. Apart from the stopping down routine, the lens itself was specially coated which, together with the use of a very fast film stock, enabled Welles to shoot scenes that had to be very brightly and elaborately lit, to a degree unheard of in the Hollywood of 1940. "Scenes which conventionally would require a shift from close-up to full shot were planned so that the action would take place simultaneously in extreme foreground and extreme background."[130]

Deep-focus had been exercised, rather haphazardly, at earlier stages in the history of the cinema. An example is to be found in Griffith's *Musketeers of Pig Alley* where the characters advance towards the camera until those in close-up are in as sharp focus as those still following in the background. But after 1925 the use of panchromatic film stock obliged cameramen to abandon deep-focus lenses in favour of "brighter" lenses; and these, when recording close-ups, tended to make everything in the background misty and out of focus. When the sensitivity of film stock improved during the Thirties, Renoir was one of the first directors to see the advantages of deep-focus. Several shots in *Boudu sauvé des eaux* (1932) and *La Règle du jeu* (1939) demonstrate this. But Welles, assuming that deep-focus presented no technical problems to a lively camera crew, systematically deployed the lens with the result that his film achieves very much the field of vision encompassed by the human eye, even to the gigantic close-ups (e.g. the lips of the dying Kane as he mumbles "Rosebud"). Toland commented in 1941: "I discovered that a 24mm lens, stopped down to f:8 or less, becomes almost literally a universal focus objective at a certain point."[131] In later films, particularly *Touch of Evil* and *The Trial,*

Xanadu and its jigsaw puzzles. Susan with Kane.

Welles was to insist on wide-angle camerawork.

The deep-focus photography throughout *Citizen Kane* is apt to echelon the characters, as it were, showing several actions—several points of interest—simultaneously. I will note five from among several examples of Welles's enrichment of the film in this way. First, when Mrs. Kane is signing the form whereby Thatcher is appointed Charles's guardian. Welles places the father at the left of the frame, the mother at the right (in close-up), with Thatcher leaning over her and, in the background, beyond the window, the boy playing in the snow. This shot is not merely economical, but it also keeps one constantly aware of the person whose future is being discussed and decided. Second, the celebration scene at the offices of the *Inquirer*. Leland and Bernstein are seated at the end of a long table with other members of the newspaper staff ranged along each side. In the background Kane is dancing with a troupe of showgirls. Suddenly he strips off his jacket and, a second or two later, tosses it towards the camera into the arms

The office celebration. Kane with dancing girls.

A shocked Bernstein reads Leland's unfinished notice to Kane (out of shot), while "The Inquirer" dramatic critic snores on.

of Leland, who is in close-up at the left of the frame. The flying jacket demonstrates the three-dimensional quality that the deep-focus lens conveys, and provides just as much of a visual shock as the objects flung "out of the screen" in the much publicised 3-D films thirteen years later. Third, when Kane finds that the besotted Leland has begun an unfavourable review of Susan's operatic *début* ("Miss Susan Alexander, a pretty but hopelessly incompetent amateur . . ."), he types out the remainder of the notice himself. Welles shows Kane at his typewriter in close-up at the left of the frame, and one sees Leland stagger down the length of the news-room (in sharp focus) towards his boss. By avoiding a series of direct cuts here, Welles counterpoints and visually extends the lull before the quarrel that seems inevitable between the two men. The sharp, deliberate tapping of Kane's machine on the "foreground" sound channel, as it were, contrasts suitably with Leland's voice in the background, and accentuates the spatial relationship.

Fourth, when Susan drugs herself in misery after her ghastly performance at the opera house, Welles conveys the implications and

Welles's use of deep-focus. Kane, in foreground, finishes Leland's notice, while Leland staggers up the length of the newsroom in protest.

urgency of the situation in one remarkable shot: in close-up are the glass and the phial of poison resorted to by Susan; in mid-shot the head of Susan, lying in shadow on the pillow; and in the background the door, beneath which a strip of light is visible. All this is given dramatic intensity by the soundtrack, with the laboured breathing of Susan and the persistent knocking of Kane on the locked door. And lastly, when Susan is practising her singing with Matisti, Welles places the piano in the foreground, with Matisti gesticulating on the left, and Susan singing pathetically on the right. Unseen by them both, Kane enters the vast room through a door in the far background. Caught in clear focus, he watches the abortive lesson; this dramatic irony again rouses a feeling of suspense, for the audience knows that Kane is about to intervene in his usual domineering manner. He is kept in sharp focus all the time as he advances towards the piano.

André Bazin, who has investigated this aspect of Welles's early work so thoroughly[41], sees in deep-focus a greater freedom for the spectator, who may choose at any one instant in the same shot the elements that intrigue him, and he underlines how much events and characters can

Kane acknowledges the crowd's applause in Madison Square Garden.

gain in ambiguity, because the significance of each moment of the action is not arbitrarily stressed. This use of deep-focus is closely allied to Welles's keenness to show how his characters can be influenced by their surroundings. For instance, Kane as a man is dwarfed by the lofty public hall (Madison Square Garden) in which he gives his election speech, but his voice and his promises are magnified and boom out over the soundtrack, creating a sense of bombast and inflated power. Similarly, Kane is often viewed from a camera set-up at floor level. This Teutonic tilt, and the corresponding exaggeration of the human figure, displays Kane's dominance over the people in his life. When Leland meets him one night in the *Inquirer* offices, only Kane's trouser leg is seen in close-up at the left of the frame while Leland sways on his feet in the background. And when Kane and Susan have one of their final quarrels, in a tent during the picnic near Xanadu, the camera views him alternately from below (as he listens to Susan's harangue, with the screaming of some outraged woman guest outside the tent providing a subtle aural aside) and from above (as he towers over Susan and tells her that he has helped her only out of love). His shadow obscures her and seemingly over-awes her. This preponderance of Kane is symbolised most discreetly in Susan's bedroom immediately before she leaves her husband. As she stands talking to Kane in mid-shot, a stuffed doll sits near the camera, in parallel profile to Susan, suggesting the true nature of her position in the eyes of Kane—that of a marionette.

Welles also uses two other common cinematic devices, creatively and incisively. The wipe, which is often so artificial, is ironically suitable for bridging the six episodes in which Welles shows the deterioration of the marriage between Kane and Emily at the breakfast table (Kane becomes gradually more and more morose, and Emily ends by reading the *Chronicle,* arch-rival of Kane's own newspaper, the *Inquirer*). Then there is one startlingly successful vertical boom shot, in the opera sequence. The camera rests on the figure of Susan, singing in rehearsal on stage; then it moves slowly upwards and at least reaches the topmost catwalk above the curtains. Two technicians look at each other, and one expresses his disapproval (there is a tribute to this shot in Truffaut's *Shoot the Piano Player,* when Fido throws his milk bomb on to the gangsters' car).

Citizen Kane is also rich in "shock images," none of which is gratuitous. The opening of the film has a sombre tone as Kane's death is disclosed in expressionistic terms, but the fade-out on the lighted window in Xanadu is succeeded abruptly by the portentous voice behind the "News on the March" credit card. Thus, within a few minutes of the start of the film, Welles has shown both the distorted, brooding image of Kane's existence, and the brash, realistic version known to the public. Another jolting cut is from Raymond's saying, "Like the time his wife left him . . ." to a close-up of a screeching white parakeet behind which, on the verandah of Xanadu, Susan walks away in high dudgeon. This visual punch represents the psychological shock sustained by Kane when he realises that Susan has gone, and explains his violent wrecking of her room. It is as though he had suffered a heart attack.

No study of *Citizen Kane* would be complete without mention of Welles's fondness for dissolves and "lightning mixes" (scenes linked by the soundtrack but not necessarily by the images). The dissolves are in evidence from the start of the film, when the camera crawls up from the "No Trespassing" sign and the wire fences dissolve into heavy gates, then into a series of views, in closer and closer proximity to the castle with—successively—a cage of monkeys, gondolas, a ghostly oriental pavilion, an abandoned golf course marker, and an open-air swimming pool in the foreground. These shots, merging swiftly one with another, convey the remote power with which Kane has hedged

Kane eats, drinks, and sleeps in the editor's room at "The Inquirer."

himself in during his life at Xanadu. The "lightning mixes" are more
plentiful and rather more difficult to catalogue. Two of the most
striking instances are (1) when, during Thatcher's recollections, the
shot changes from his wishing the young Kane "A merry Christmas—"
to the same man, somewhat older, continuing the sentence, "—and a
prosperous New Year" just before his *protégé's* twenty-fifth birthday;
and (2) when Kane's clapping at Susan Alexander's piano recital in
her own room is dovetailed into the applause from a small crowd as
Leland campaigns for Kane to be Governor in the 1916 elections, and
then almost immediately afterwards Leland's sentence, "—who entered
upon this campaign . . ." is replaced by that of Kane himself (a second
later) in the huge hall, ". . . with one purpose only." This dramatic
continuity illustrates Kane's frightening and yet brittle rise to power,
while Bernard Herrmann's score, now baleful, now cheerful, is keenly
appropriate.

But *Citizen Kane* is important for its basic construction as well as
for the myriad details that comprise its technical grammar. Flashbacks
were used often before 1940—perhaps Carné's *Le Jour se lève* explored
their advantages most thoroughly—but Welles was the first director to
use them not merely at random but so as to present five biased views
of one person. The memories of Thatcher, Bernstein, Leland, Susan,
and Raymond, while carefully arranged in chronological order, are all
slightly prejudiced. "Each major flashback begins at a later point in
time than its predecessor, but each flashback overlaps with at least one
of the others, so that the same event or period is seen from two or
three points of view."[121] For instance, Susan's *début* in *Salammbô* at
the Chicago Opera House is seen three times altogether in the film,
in the newsreel, in Leland's flashback when it is seen at rehearsal
through his bored eyes in the dress circle, and in Susan's own
memories when the audience exists in a black, hostile void beyond
the glaring footlights. This gives the episode an additional narrative
dimension, which is reflected spatially in the lighting and camerawork.

Moreover, these recollections are not marred by the customary aura
of age and remoteness, because Welles has so cunningly summarized
Kane's obituary in the nine-minute newsreel. Several incidents covered
by the "News on the March" bulletin are made to look grainy and
shaky, as though loaned by some archive, and yet later in the film the
same shots appear in the course of the flashbacks—in crystal *clear* vision.
Thus Welles causes events literally to come to life in the flashbacks
(the shot of Susan and Kane climbing into a carriage after their wedding, for example) . Welles himself recalls that when the film opened
in Italy just after the war, a lot of people booed and hissed and even

shook their fists at the projection box because they thought the newsreel material was sheer bad photography.† The newsreel has a further significance in that it provides a salient outline of Kane's life and enables Welles to dispense with a strictly logical narrative style. As Joseph McBride has written, "A system has been created in which all of Kane's actions are now in the past tense—and hence no longer of any effect. The events of his life as we will see them exist in a limbo of moral futility."[106]

Apart from anything else, the news digest is a wickedly accurate parody of Louis de Rochemont's "March of Time" series, then at the height of its fame. The use of titles as well as a commentary, the authoritative paternalism of the announcer, music oscillating between the grandiloquent and the sublime, and the bombastic language ("Then, last week, as it must to all men, death came to Charles Foster Kane") catch the familiar traits of newsreels like "March of Time" and Hearst's own "News of the Day," which were as widely seen and revered by the masses in the Thirties as Rank's "Look at Life" was in Britain in the Fifties and Sixties.

★   ★   ★

The form of *Citizen Kane,* superficially so haphazard, is in reality tightly constructed. Practically every movement has its complement at another point in the film. Apart from the opening and closing scenes, when the camera begins and ends by focusing in close-up on the "No Trespassing" sign outside Xanadu, one can quote the crane shot that climbs up, over the roof, and down to the skylight of the El Rancho night club in Atlantic City (an immaculate dissolve gives the impression that the camera probes down to the table where Susan is sitting). When Thompson first arrives, the neon sign "Susan Alexander—Cabaret" is flashing; when he returns much later in the film and much later in time, the sign is out, signifying the decline in Susan's fortunes since Kane's death. A French critic has noted that the shot is also "the physical image of that violation of consciences and intimacy that the press has perpetrated and that *Citizen Kane* seeks both to represent and to attack."[52]

Nearly all the players in *Citizen Kane* were unknown when the film appeared. Oddly, few of them have established a major reputation over the years. Joseph Cotten still plays the occasional lead; Agnes Moorehead and Everett Sloane (until his death in 1965) have appeared in minor parts, though always with distinction; Erskine Sanford (Carter in this film) was seen to somewhat better effect as the judge

Emily (Ruth Warrick) and Kane Jr. (Sonny Bupp) listen to Kane in Madison Square Garden.

in *The Lady from Shanghai;* and Ray Collins had a late-flowering success on TV as Lt. Tragg in the Perry Mason series. Nearly all these actors and actresses had worked with Welles in his Mercury Theatre group, and the performances in *Citizen Kane* are as near perfect as can be. Welles himself has never had a role since that suits his capacity as well as Kane does. His first appearance, brash in braces and open-necked shirt, and swinging on his chair as he simultaneously lights his pipe and rebuffs the protests of Walter Thatcher, oozes the almost pardonable arrogance that is the making of Kane's career. Never once does Welles lose the magnetic aura that Kane seems to carry about him like a divine right of kings, even in old age (the make-up staff of RKO succeeded remarkably in making the twenty-five-year-old Welles look at least sixty in certain sequences). He has that supremely self-confident air of one who knows in advance what his detractors will say and then disarms them with a single witticism or command.

Citizen Kane remains Welles's finest film, a treasury of cinematic metaphors and devices, and a portrait of an incredibly dramatic per-

Outside the rally: Kane and Emily.

sonality. The theme of the life of a grandiose figure ending in tragedy
is the blueprint for nearly all Welles's subsequent work (*The Stranger,
The Lady from Shanghai, Macbeth, Othello, Confidential Report,
Touch of Evil, Chimes at Midnight, The Immortal Story*). Irrespective
of the fluctuations of critical opinion (and in both the 1962 and 1972
Sight and Sound polls it emerged as the film cited most by critics asked
to name the ten best films ever made), it will remain one of the few
films of which the long-term influence on the history of the cinema
was as remarkable as its initial impact.

Kane wants to know why "The Inquirer" has not scooped its rival paper's lead story.

Script Extract

CITIZEN KANE

LELAND (*to the reporter Thompson on the terrace of the nursing home*) : She was like all the girls I knew in dancing school. Very nice girls, very nice. Emily was a little nicer. Well, after the first couple of months she and Charlie didn't see much of each other—except at breakfast. It was a marriage just like any other marriage.
Slow dissolve to the Kanes' apartment. Music. The dining room. Leland is visible for a few moments more, continuing his narration. The passage of time is indicated by a series of wipes.
Emily is sitting down, and to the right of the frame Kane enters and approaches his wife, a serviette over his arm, plates in his hand. He kisses her on the forehead, puts the plates on the table and sits down next to her.
EMILY: Charles . . .
KANE: You're beautiful.
EMILY: Oh, I can't be.
KANE: Yes, you are, you're very, very beautiful.
The camera moves into close-medium shot.
EMILY: I've never been to six parties in one night—
KANE: Extremely beautiful.
EMILY: —in all my life. I've never even been up this late.
KANE: It's a matter of habit.
EMILY: I wonder what the servants will think.
KANE: They'll think we enjoyed ourselves.
EMILY: Dear . . .
KANE: Didn't we?
EMILY: I don't see why you have to go straight off to the newspaper.
KANE: You never should have married a newspaper man—they're worse than sailors . . . (*pause*) . . . I absolutely adore you.
EMILY: Oh, Charles, even newspaper men have to sleep!
Medium close-up of Kane looking to right foreground. Music.
KANE: I'll call Mr. Bernstein and have him put off my appointments until noon.

Medium close-up of Emily smiling . . . and successive close-ups of each of them as they talk.
KANE: What time is it?
EMILY: Oh, I don't know, it's late.
KANE: It's early!
The camera pans . . . Dissolve.
Pan that comes to a halt on Emily seated at a table behind a vase full of flowers.
EMILY: Charles . . . do you know how long you kept me waiting last night?
Kane, seated on the other side of the flowers, stares towards the foreground.
EMILY (*off*): —while you went to the newspaper for ten minutes?
Emily looks through the flowers towards the foreground.
EMILY: What do you *do* on a newspaper in the middle of the night?
KANE (*off*): Emily . . .
Shot of Kane on the other side of the table putting out a match.
KANE: My dear, your only co-respondent is the *Inquirer*.
EMILY (*off*): Sometimes I think . . . (*Dissolve*)
Medium close-up and pan on Emily seated at table.
EMILY: . . . I'd prefer a rival of flesh and blood.
KANE (*off*): Oh, Emily!
Kane, on the other side of the flowers, frowns.
KANE: I don't spend that much time on the newspaper.
EMILY: It isn't just the time . . . It's what you print. Attacking—
Pause. Change of shot.
EMILY (*off*): —the President.
KANE (*smiling*): You mean Uncle John.
EMILY: I mean the President of the United States.
KANE (*off*): He's still Uncle John . . . and he's still a well-meaning fathead—
EMILY (*off*): Charles!
KANE: —who's letting a pack of high-pressure crooks run his administration.
KANE (*off*): This whole oil scandal . . .
EMILY: He happens to be the President, Charles, not you.
KANE: That's a mistake that will be corrected one of these days.
EMILY (*off*): Your Mr. Bernstein . . .
Dissolve.
Shot of Emily. Music.
EMILY: . . . sent Junior the most incredible atrocity yesterday, Charles. I simply can't have it . . .

Kane is at table eating his breakfast and lays down his knife and fork.
EMILY (*off*): . . . in the nursery.
Shot of Kane frowning.
KANE: Mr. Bernstein is apt to pay a visit to the nursery now and then.
EMILY: Does he have to?
KANE: Yes.
EMILY (*off*): Really, Charles . . .
Dissolve.
Camera, after a zip-pan, focuses on Emily at table. She is older and rather more wrinkled.
EMILY: People will think . . .
Shot of Kane frowning as he holds a cup of coffee in mid-air.
KANE: What I tell them to think!
Dissolve.
Camera, after a zip-pan, focuses on Emily at table again. She looks into the foreground, then begins reading a newspaper again. It is the Chronicle. *Seated opposite her, Kane has a newspaper spread out in front of him. He glances into the foreground, and then lowers his eyes to the paper (the* Inquirer). *Reverse travelling shot shows Emily seated at the right of the table. Camera withdraws and a dissolve reveals Leland again in the nursing home.*

Climax of the breakfast sequence.

CITIZEN KANE

Scene: a street at night. Kane and Emily stand in front of a house. A light shines behind the door. The bell rings while they wait.
KANE: I had no idea you had this flair for melodrama, Emily.

A shadow appears behind the glass of the door, and a maid opens it.
MAID: Come right in, Mr. Kane!

The maid stands aside. Emily goes in. Kane follows her. The maid shuts the door. Fade.

Inside the house. Mid-shot of the hall. Low-angle shot looking towards the stair-rail and the landing above. A door at the back opens. Susan appears as Kane and Emily ascend the stairs in the foreground.
SUSAN: Charlie!

Kane and Emily look up towards her and continue to climb the stairs. The camera follows them and they stop near Susan's door.
SUSAN: Charlie! He forced me to send your wife that letter. I didn't want to. He's been sayin' the most terrible . . .

Gettys appears in the doorway.
GETTYS: Good evening, Mrs. Kane. I don't suppose anybody'll introduce us. I'm Jim Gettys.
EMILY: Yes.

Gettys takes a step back. Emily moves into the apartment.
GETTYS: I made Miss—Miss Alexander send you the note, Mrs. Kane. She didn't want to at first—
SUSAN: I—
GETTYS: —but she did it!
SUSAN: Charlie, the things he said to me. He threatened . . .

Kane, furious, strides towards Gettys inside the room.
KANE: Gettys . . .

The camera withdraws from the two men. Susan goes out of frame. Emily is inside the room.
KANE: . . . I don't think I will postpone doing something about you until I'm elected. To start with, I think I'll break your neck.

GETTYS: Maybe you can do it and maybe you can't, Mr. Kane.

Gettys retreats towards the back of the room and goes out of frame. Kane walks towards him and stops.

EMILY: Charles!

Kane turns towards Emily as she speaks.

EMILY: Your breaking this man's neck would scarcely explain (*pause*) this note.

She lowers her eyes and begins to read.

EMILY: ". . . serious consequences for Mr. Kane, for yourself, and for your son."

Susan appears at left.

SUSAN: He just wanted to get her to come here.

EMILY: What does this note mean, Miss . . .

SUSAN: I'm Susan Alexander. I know what you think, Mrs. Kane.

EMILY: What does this note mean, Miss Alexander?

Kane turns away. Emily turns to her right.

GETTYS: She don't know, Mrs. Kane.

Pan on to Gettys in the background. Kane starts to move toward him.

GETTYS: She just sent it because I made her see it wouldn't be smart for her not to send it.

KANE: In case you don't know, Emily, this "gentleman" . . .

GETTYS: I'm not a gentleman. Your husband's only trying to be funny calling me one. I don't even know what a gentleman is. You see my idea of a gentleman—huh!—*He approaches Emily.*

GETTYS: Well, Mrs. Kane, if I owned a newspaper, and I didn't like the way somebody was doing things—some politician, say—I'd fight him with everything I had. Only I wouldn't show him in a convict suit with stripes so his children could see the picture in the papers . . . or his mother . . .

KANE: You're a cheap crooked grafter, and your concern for your children and your mother—

Gettys turn again towards Kane who is at the back of the room.

GETTYS: We're talking now about what you are! Mrs. Kane, I'm fighting for my life. Not just my political life, my life.

Susan approaches Kane.

SUSAN: Charlie, he said unless you withdrew your name, he says he'd tell everybody . . .

GETTYS: That's what I said.

EMILY: You mean—

GETTYS (*continuing*): Here's the chance I'm willing to give him. It's more of a chance than he'd give me. Unless Mr. Kane makes up his mind by tomorrow he's so sick he has to go away for a year or two, Monday morning, every paper in this state—except his—will carry the story I'm going to give them.

EMILY: What story?

GETTYS: The story about him and Miss Alexander, Mrs. Kane.
Susan turns towards Gettys.

SUSAN: There isn't any story . . .

GETTYS: Shut up!

SUSAN: Mr. Kane's just . . .

GETTYS: We've got evidence that'd look bad in the headlines. (*He turns to Kane.*) Do you want me to *give* you the evidence, Mr. Kane? (*He turns now to Emily.*) I'd rather Mr. Kane withdrew without *having* to get the story published. Not that I care about him, but I'd be better off . . .

SUSAN: But what about—

GETTYS (*pause*) : . . . so would you, Mrs. Kane.

SUSAN: And what about me? Charlie, he said my name'd be dragged through the mud . . . that everywhere I went from now on—

EMILY: There seems to be only one decision you can make, Charles. I'd say it had been made for you.

KANE: You can't tell me the voters of this state . . .

EMILY: I'm not interested in the voters of this state right now . . .

Mid-shot of Kane in the right foreground. Gettys and the two women are at the other end of the room.

EMILY: . . . I'm interested in our son.

SUSAN: Charlie, if they publish the story . . .

EMILY: They won't. (*Pause.*) Goodnight, Mr. Gettys.

She turns and moves towards the door, then turns again to look at Kane, whose face is in shadow.

EMILY: Are you coming, Charles?

KANE: No.

Panning shot: Gettys and Susan are in the foreground. Kane moves slowly towards them and stops.

KANE: I'm staying here.

Pan so that Emily and Kane face each other on either side of the frame.

KANE: I can fight this all alone.

EMILY (*off-screen now*) : Charles . . .

Gettys is in the background to the left. Emily, facing the camera, is in the foreground.

EMILY: . . . if you don't listen to reason, it may be too late.

KANE: Too late? (*He advances out of the shadow at the back of the room.*) For what? For you and this (*glances aside at Gettys*) public thief to take the love of the people of this state away from me?

SUSAN: Charlie, you got other things to think about. Your little boy. You don't want him to read about you in the papers.

KANE: There's only one person in the world to decide what I'm going to do, and that's me.

Shot of Emily, from between Kane and Gettys, in the background.

EMILY: You decided what you were going to do, Charles, some time ago.

She goes through the door and out of frame.

GETTYS: You're making a bigger fool of yourself than I thought you would, Mr. Kane.

KANE: I've got nothing to talk to you about!

GETTYS: You're licked. Why don't you . . . ?

KANE: Get out! If you want to see me have the warden write me a letter.

GETTYS: If it was anybody else I'd say what's going to happen to you would be a lesson to you. Only you're going to need more than one lesson, and you're going to get more than one lesson.

KANE: Don't worry about me, Gettys.

Gettys dons his hat, goes through the door and out of frame. Kane follows him, crying out. Susan, at right, in the foreground, remains stunned.

KANE: Don't worry about me! I'm Charles Foster Kane! I'm no cheap crooked politician . . .

He rushes to the bannisters, still shouting.

KANE: . . . trying to save himself . . .

The camera is at the far end of the landing. High angle shot on the well of the stairs. Kane stumbles down some stairs, shouting as he goes. Gettys, lower down, keeps descending as though nothing were happening.

KANE: . . . from the consequences of his crimes!

Kane grasps the bannister and watches Gettys, who continues to walk downstairs. His voice becomes almost a scream.

KANE: Gettys!

Close-up of Gettys arriving at the foot of the stairs, a slight smile on his face. He goes out of frame at the left. Kane leans over the bannister and continues screaming.

KANE: I'm going to send you to . . .

Close-up of Kane shouting into the camera.

KANE: Sing-Sing!

As he says this Susan comes running out on to the upper landing.

KANE: . . . Sing-Sing, Gettys!

In front of the house, Emily is standing at the right near the door. Gettys comes out and starts closing the door.

KANE (*off-screen*): Sing-Sing!

Gettys shuts the door and doffs his hat.

GETTYS: Have you a car, Mrs. Kane?

EMILY: Yes, thank you.

GETTYS: Goodnight.

EMILY: Goodnight.

Emily leaves the frame at right. Music. Gettys, in his turn, leaves the frame at left. The camera travels back from the door. Fade-out.

THE MAGNIFICENT AMBERSONS

"It was so advanced, so ahead of its time, that people just didn't understand it"—MARK ROBSON[118]

PLOT OUTLINE— Isabel Amberson, a member of an important family in Indianapolis at the end of the Nineteenth century, marries Wilbur Minafer. She is really in love with Eugene Morgan, a designer of automobiles who is despised by the family for his bourgeois background. Twenty years later Wilbur dies, leaving Isabel, with her son George, to live alone in the Amberson mansion with her father, her brother, and her sister-in-law Fanny. She has again fallen in love with Eugene (now also a widower whose daughter Lucy is being courted by George), but George intervenes and prevents Eugene from seeing his mother. Isabel goes away on a long trip in an effort to forget her lover, and George's pride prevents him from marrying the daughter of a man he dislikes so much. Eventually Isabel dies unhappily, and her father follows soon afterwards. Fanny and George have to leave the family house, and George is involved in a motoring accident. In hospital he asks Eugene for forgiveness.

IN THE AFTERMATH OF CITIZEN KANE, a success with most critics but hardly a box-office triumph, Welles apparently wanted to shoot *The Pickwick Papers* (with W. C. Fields), but the project did not reach fruition, like so many of his subsequent plans (see list of unfinished projects at the end of this book). Instead, in a mere nine months, Welles wrote an imaginative screenplay of Booth Tarkington's 1919 Pulitzer Prize-winning novel, *The Magnificent Ambersons*. Already in late 1939 he had played with Walter Huston in a radio version of the story.

The film of *The Magnificent Ambersons* was begun on October 28,

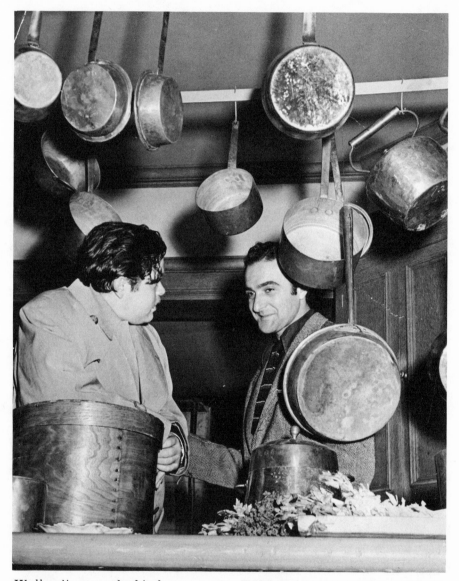

Welles discusses the kitchen scene for THE MAGNIFICENT AMBER-
SONS *with cinematographer Stanley Cortez.*

1941, and shooting finished at the RKO Studios at the end of January, 1942. Welles was then sent to Brazil to make *It's All True* (see Appendix) and the editing was taken out of his hands. "Five, maybe six, reels of *Ambersons* are exactly as I cut them before leaving for South America, with the exception of a single cut in the middle of a very long travelling shot. The cut involved a couple of remarks about 'olives'—a novelty in the town. Don't ask me why they wanted it out. The result was a useless jump in an otherwise unbroken scene. I also cut the last part of *Ambersons,* but it was completely re-done after a preview. About forty-five minutes were cut out—the whole heart of the picture really—for which the first part had been a preparation. The closing sequence in the hospital was written and directed by somebody else. It bears no relation to my script."† Mark Robson, who worked with Robert Wise on the editing (under the supervision of Jack Moss, Welles's agent-cum-executive producer), talks of some ten to fifteen previews. "At least an hour was taken out of release, although I don't recall specific sequences. It was a kind of chopped-down version of Orson's original conception."[118]

So *The Magnificent Ambersons* is a true *film maudit,* like Stroheim's *Greed.* The result is frustrating, to say the least. Parts of the firm are remarkable for the subtlety of the style and the unparalleled brilliance of the acting (has anyone in American films ever reached such a pitch of intensity as Agnes Moorehead does in her hysterical scenes with Tim Holt?). But the latter part of the film is full of illogicalities (e.g. the sudden softening in George's attitude), and the continuity is often vulgar and abrupt. A minor irritation is the fact that Eugene looks younger in the final shots than he does twenty years earlier in time. But in spite of its imperfections, *The Magnificent Ambersons* beguiles ever more *cinéphiles,* and was placed eighth in the 1972 *Sight and Sound* poll for best film of all time.

★   ★   ★

The film is—quite unashamedly—nostalgic in tone, and is thus in striking contrast to the rest of Welles's work. The frame is rimmed with soft focus, giving each shot the look of a faded photograph, and the opening sequence demonstrates Welles's affection for a lost era. "The Magnificence of the Ambersons began in 1873," he narrates behind a black screen; then the camera opens and the darkness dissolves into a view of the Amberson mansion. Quaint customs and habits are dwelt upon: the streetcar, "too slow for us nowadays—because the faster we're carried the less time we have to spare"; high-top boots, soon replaced by shoes and Congress gaiters; "that prettiest of all vanished customs, the serenade," with Eugene Morgan playing to attract Isabel Amberson and collapsing on his instrument in the process; and the stove-pipe hat, worn by Wilbur Minafer as he takes Isabel out for a row on the lake. "In those days, they had time for everything," continues Welles, letting fall a moment later the information that Isabel is to marry Wilbur, even though her heart lies with Eugene.

Thus in a few minutes of running time the background and the situation have been brought into line with the leading characters, with a lucidity that recalls the newsreel at the start of *Citizen Kane*. But in *The Magnificent Ambersons* Welles's touch is gentler at every point, as if in deference to a distant epoch and a great family. Not that the style of the film is sentimental or insipid; it is merely less obtrusive when key issues have to be stressed. On one level *The Magnificent Ambersons* meanders unhurriedly on its way, a faithful reflection of the pace of life at the turn of the century (although this is not to be confused with the overall slackness of the film's structure, which might

Pushing in the snow. Dolores Costello, Agnes Moorehead, Joseph Cotten, and Ray Collins.

have been tightened had Welles edited it himself). But on a more profound level, it shows a conflict as bitter and as important as those treated by Welles in his other films. There is a struggle in Indianapolis between a landed aristocracy fast drifting into decadence, and an industrial bourgeoisie anxious to gain control of society.

In *The Magnificent Ambersons,* Georgie Minafer is the last bastion of this aristocracy, and Eugene Morgan is the representative of the industrial pioneers. In the material sense, the conflict is epitomised in the growth of the automobile at the expense of the horse and carriage, and Welles manages to compress it into one memorable winter scene. George and Lucy whirl along gaily in their horse-drawn sledge while Eugene's motor-carriage lies helplessly bogged in the snow. Suddenly they pass Eugene, everyone appears in a single shot, and George calls out, "Get a horse! Get a horse!" It is the cry of a man clinging with almost desperate confidence to the outworn symbol of his society. And George's humiliation is dwelt upon by Welles as his sledge spills him and Lucy into a drift; in the end he is forced to push Eugene's car along, receiving a face full of fumes for his pains while the others start to sing "The Man Who Broke the Bank at Monte Carlo." Snow here, as much as in *Citizen Kane* and *Chimes at Midnight,* carries a nostalgic charge. Significantly, Welles irises out on the car as it crosses the horizon and the screen's blackness gives way to a man's shadow on the glass door of the Amberson mansion. Wilbur Minafer is dead.

★　　★　　★

In the majority of Welles's films the limelight falls on only one or two characters (Othello and Iago, Arkadin, Raina and Van Stratten, Quinlan and Vargas, Joseph K, Leni and the Advocate, Falstaff and the Prince) but in *The Magnificent Ambersons* Welles studies no fewer that seven people in detail. Each of them ingeniously affects the outcome of the film. Georgie Minafer, egotism incarnate, is the villain. From his childhood he has been regarded as "a princely terror" and everyone in the town longs to see him receive his "comeuppance." There is an amusing scene in which he fights with the son of the local lawyer, Bronson, and then rounds on the father when he intervenes (one is reminded acutely of the rebelliousness of the youthful Kane when confronted by Thatcher in the snow). Then, in his early twenties, at the ball in the Amberson mansion, he strolls arm in arm with Lucy Morgan, cutting her father dead, ignoring the interjections of his Uncle Jack, and making rude remarks about the other "young ducks" with whom Lucy seems to be acquainted. Later, one sees his

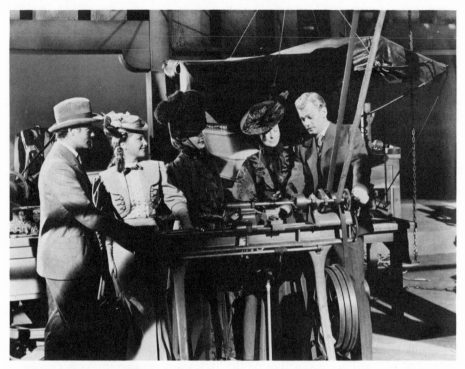

Eugene Morgan (Joseph Cotten, at right) shows the Ambersons his automobile plant.

lack of feeling in the kitchen scene with Fanny. Serviette tucked into his collar, he eats gluttonously while passing sly, teasing comments about Fanny's fondness for Eugene Morgan. At the dinner table one day he suddenly says in an audible voice, "Automobiles are a useless nuisance," in a deliberate attempt to upset Eugene, whose entire life is devoted to the development of the motor car. When he discovers from Fanny that Eugene is really courting his widowed mother, he refuses to allow him to enter the hall: "You're not wanted in this house, Mr. Morgan, now or at any other time." The bitterness in George's character is aggravated by the fact that he is in love with Eugene's daughter Lucy; love for her and love for his mother fight for dominance within him, and his ultimate tragedy is that by rejecting Eugene he dashes not merely his mother's life but also his own, for Lucy is faithful to her father. This inner anguish is beautifully captured by Welles in a close-up shot of George's face reflected in the window pane as he watches Eugene leave the mansion for the last time. Georgie can never quite forgive Eugene (even though the final scene, not shot by Welles, would lead one to believe so) but he does forgive

Isabel. His earlier, outraged protest, "But you're my mother, you're an Amberson!" changes to shame and misery as he kneels beside Isabel's bed long after her death, in the dim deserted mansion. Quietly, the narration begins: "Something had happened. A thing which years ago had been the eagerest hope of many, many good citizens of the town. And now it came at last. George Amberson Minafer had got his come-uppance. He'd got it three times filled and running over." Ironically, he has both his legs broken in a serious "automobile accident" shortly afterwards (enter Bernard Herrmann's brooding, ominous chords). George is a very human character. One can understand his reactions even if one cannot sympathise with him. But without doubt he belongs to the scorpions of Welles's world; like Kane, like Arkadin, like Quinlan, he irritates and blights the lives of those around him almost in spite of himself.

Eugene is the complete antithesis of George. Gentle, kind, and remarkably tolerant, he never acts vindictively against this upstart who destroys his relationship with Isabel. The opening sequence of the film reveals how he is passed over by the family in favour of the more respectable Wilbur Minafer, and he does not appear again until

Luncheon at the Amberson mansion.

eighteen years have elapsed, and the last great ball in honour of Georgie's sophomore, takes place at the Amberson mansion. Now a widower, he is obviously still in love with Isabel, and she with him. But George attacks him unceasingly and, paradoxically, for the wrong reasons. He believes that Eugene is trying to extort money from old Major Amberson to finance his "horseless carriage," and that he dresses up specially to impress Fanny. He even thinks that Eugene will not let his daughter marry him until he goes into business and earns a steady livelihood.

The tolerance in Eugene's character is shown most notably in the dining room scene, when George insults the entire conception of automobiles. While Jack and the Major rebuke their relative, Eugene philosophises on the growth of the invention. "It may be that they won't add to the beauty of the world or the life of men's souls . . . They're going to alter war and they're going to alter peace"; this willingness to admit the dangers of his pursuit arouses sympathy for the man and for his position in a society that does not countenance progress.* With the same open mind he accepts the failure of his romance with Isabel, and writes her a letter of consolation before she leaves on her world trip. "Don't strike my life down twice, dear. This time I've not deserved it."

Isabel herself is an even more harmless person, never unfaithful to Wilbur throughout their long marriage and more dismayed than infuriated by her son's rebellious attitude. "She's kind of a delightful young lady," says an onlooker at the beginning of the film, and even in middle age Isabel retains a distinguished beauty. Her love for Eugene is never overstressed by Welles; instead it is discernible in moments like the leavetaking after the ball when, in shadow, they say a simple goodnight to each other amid a babble of voices. Eventually, she pines away. One thinks of Hemingway's dictum, "If two people love each other, there can be no happy end to it." George and Uncle Jack do Eugene the ultimate injustice; they prevent him, however gently, from seeing her as she is about to die.

By contrast with her, Isabel's sister-in-law Fanny is far more prone

---

* Welles was asked about his father in a BBC *Monitor* (1960) programme: "He retired! . . . early in his life, having been an automobile manufacturer as in *Magnificent Ambersons*—he was one of the first in the world, the first in America and one of the first automobile racers, and he gave it up, however, taking the view that automobiles were a passing phase, just as they were becoming very big, and went into the manufacture of bicycle lamps—on which he made a fortune. . . . He was also a playboy, bon viveur, he was a great friend of Mr. Hearst's—among other things—and of Booth Tarkington's, who wrote the novel on which *Magnificent Ambersons* was based. So there's a very close connection in both films to my father."

The last great ball at the Amberson mansion. Above: George and Lucy, Fanny and Wilbur, with an old friend. Below: Eugene waltzes amid the shadows with Isabel while George and Lucy watch from the stairs.

to violent outbursts. She adores Eugene, but never declares her love for him because she feels that Isabel and Eugene are made for each other. This sentiment, combined with resentment at the way George treats her ("Oh, you're always picking on me! Always. Ever since you were a little boy! . . . But it's only poor old Fanny Minafer!") builds up inside her to a pitch of self-pity that floods out in two climactic scenes, the first, on the stairs, in which she tells George about his mother's love for Eugene in a way that smacks rather of jealousy on her part, and the second, among the shrouded furniture of the mansion, when she collapses in front of George in anguish at the dissolution of the old family home. For Fanny more than for anyone in the film, the Amberson way of life has become an integral part of her own existence and the cooking a genuine pleasure. There is tragedy in a minor key towards the end when she admits to Georgie between sobs that she has invested her money foolishly. Only $28 remain; the boarding house accommodation costs $36 a month and $22.50 for dinner. Georgie, as destitute as Fanny, has to abandon his career in the law to earn the money. Thanks mainly to Agnes Moorehead's superb acting, Fanny is as memorable a character as any in *The Magnificent*

Fanny (Agnes Moorehead) is defeated by Isabel's death and George's behaviour.

Ambersons, a creature ruled by her instincts, revelling in the Indian summer of a respected family, with a dream of bridge and gossip to follow.

The only other female personality in the film is Lucy Morgan. Her role, one feels, must have suffered from the drastic cutting behind Welles's back, because certain scenes show her to be a girl of a maturity beyond her years, a girl capable of deep emotions and an understanding of those emotions; just what might be expected, in fact, in any daughter of Eugene's. Courted in proprietorial style by George at the Amberson ball, she refuses to be drawn into criticism of her acquaintances or, as happens later, into an acceptance of his marriage proposal. Thereafter, she participates in only two sequences of any importance. The first is when George, about to leave for a trip with his mother, says goodbye to Lucy, and hopes fervently that she will join with him against her own father. She faces all his hesitant, embarrassed remarks with a fixed smile. Puzzled, he leaves her. "I think it's goodbye for good, Lucy." The camera dwells on Lucy, and one sees her eyes brim with tears and the smile change to anguish like a mime shorn of his mask. This hidden melancholy also underlies her last scene, with Eugene in the garden, as she recounts the Indian folk tale that so cunningly parallels the story of the Ambersons. George has ruined his life, but instead of resorting to revenge, Lucy falls back happily on her beloved home life. "I had too much unpleasant excitement," she says to Eugene. "I don't want any more. In fact, I don't want anything but you."

Major Amberson is a reticent man and yet sets his imprint on the last years of the Ambersons with considerable force. He outlives his daughter Isabel, and the scene of his own death (like Henry IV's in *Chimes at Midnight*) is among the most haunting in the film. "And now," narrates Welles with a tender respect, "Major Amberson was engaged in the profoundest thinking of his life. And he realised that everything which had worried him or delighted him during this lifetime was all trifling and waste beside what concerned him now . . . how to enter an unknown country where he was not even sure of being recognised as an Amberson."

The old man is seen in close-up, with a light from the drawing room fire flickering across his pensive face. He ponders on the source of life: "Must be the sun," he muses, "earth came out o' the sun, and we came out o' the earth." It is splendidly reminiscent of the opening reel of Dovzhenko's *Earth,* where the old father dies amid his relatives, lying against a tree, a peaceful smile on his lips. It belongs among those brief intervals of simplicity that one can find in all of Welles's work

George bids a blunt farewell to Lucy (Anne Baxter).

(Quinlan's meeting with Tanya, for example, or Othello's embracing Desdemona—"Come, I have but an hour of love with thee").

Jack Amberson, Isabel's brother, forms an interesting contrast with the materialistic greed of Georgie; he seems almost a kinsman of Eugene Morgan, except that his reproaches carry a little more asperity, and his engaging mixture of politeness and outspokenness is best in evidence at that odd little station scene when he entrains in an attempt to earn some money to bolster the declining fortunes of the Ambersons. With the glass of the station looming dimly behind him, he manages to tell George in a most effective manner that he thinks him an adulterated swine. But he's aware of more timeless considerations. "Ah, life and money both behave like loose quicksilver in a nest of cracks. When they're gone, you can't tell where, or what you did with them," he says, recalling how he said goodbye to a pretty girl at the old "Depot."

Georgie is left, presumably, to ruminate on his own tactlessness compared with his Uncle's behaviour; Jack Amberson would tease Fanny about Eugene like anyone else, but he would not go so far as to insult Eugene at the dinner table about his principal passion in

The station scene: Jack Amberson (Ray Collins) with George.

life. He remains in one's memory as a token of the fine breeding that must have distinguished the Ambersons in their heyday.

The Magnificent Ambersons is not, then, a portrait in depth of one man, as are so many of Welles's films.* It is rather the study of an entire town, and each of the characters (even those who, like Wilbur Minafer and Mrs. Johnson, live innocuously in the background) represents a different shade of opinion and decorum. The style of the film itself aims at a similar end. The offscreen narration, which was virtually new to the feature film in 1942 (although it recalls the convention of the silent cinema's explanatory titles), establishes an intimacy that is counterpointed visually by the shots of the neighbours gossiping as Eugene tries to court Isabel and by the long travelling shot that accompanies George and Lucy in their carriage as they ride through the town and the polished shop windows reflect buildings and people on the other side of the street. The gay tempo of life in the

---

* "*Ambersons* was a very happy experience for me because it's the only film I have ever made in which I didn't have to appear—it was a joy not to have to stand in front of a camera." (Welles in a BBC *Monitor* interview)

closing years of the century is expressed in the jaunty pieces of music that link these early sequences, and in the brilliant climax to the long stroll of George and Lucy through the Amberson mansion on the night of the ball, when Lucy, exasperated by her partner's disdain for all professional men, asks him what he intends to be. "A yachtsman!" he replies fatuously, and the pair dance away into the background of the shot while Welles fades the image to an almost still-life shot of the huge ball; Isabel and Eugene dance serenely to the last violinist's strains.

Side by side with this impish streak in the style is a great restraint that emerges in such scenes as the death of Wilbur Minafer (one is never shown the coffin—a wreath on the big oak door and a silent ring of faces round the bier are sufficient), or George's final journey—"He walked home slowly through what seemed to be the strange streets of a strange city. This was the last walk he was to take up National Avenue . . . Tomorrow they would move out." The narrator's voice in a film has been misused *ad infinitum* by Hollywood since Welles mastered it so effectively. The experiments with sound are less flamboyant in *The Magnificent Ambersons* than they are in *Kane*—but they are most subtle. By merging several tracks at once Welles achieves the babble of voices that lends such conviction to the leavetaking at the Amberson ball and the excursion in the snow. Welles was a pioneer in this important field; he was the first to realise, although a man of the theatre himself, that the cinema could not adhere to the theatrical fallacy that people invariably wait for one person to finish his speech before interrupting.

Stanley Cortez's sophisticated photography always emphasises the interplay of light and shade in Welles's vision. One remembers too the deep shadows round the parting guests after the ball, or round George and his mother as they discuss Wilbur's failing health. As Eugene and Lucy talk beneath a tree in the garden, their faces are marked by sombre, foreboding shadows. Darkness seems eager to invade the Amberson mansion, as it does Macbeth's castle and the town of Los Robles in *Touch of Evil*. While she reads Eugene's final letter, Isabel looks physically trapped within the darkened room.

The scene to which Welles devoted most attention is, superficially, the simplest—the scene in the kitchen when George, and then Jack, teases Fanny about her love for Eugene Morgan. "We built a set," recalled Welles in an interview on the BBC *Monitor* programme in 1960. "You may notice how the camera never moves—there's a very slight pan—the camera itself never moves. The actors were rehearsed for five weeks before we started the film. And on this scene at least four days, except that this scene was never written. No word of it was written—and we discussed everybody's life, each one's character, their background, their position at this moment in the story, what they would think about everything—and then sat down and cranked the camera and every actor made up his lines as he went along. The scene lasts three and a half minutes or something in its entirety [*actually a few seconds over four minutes—PDC*] and was written by the actors as we went along. I'm very proud of them for it. It has an extraordinary effect, entirely due to their work and their preparation for doing it." This reluctance to fragment the scene is in direct opposition to classical montage; Welles prefers to show the genuine duration of an event or a conversation without forcing it to comply with an abstract form of time. Throughout the film he uses dissolves and fades rather than direct cuts so as to preserve the impression of each scene and to make the film as a whole more fluent and intense.

Frame blow-up from the kitchen sequence, as Jack and George tease Fanny.

The Amberson mansion is a perfect physical symbol of the family's outlook and way of life. The broad staircases, the high ceilings, and the bedrooms that reflect the personalities of their occupants, impinge on all the scenes played within the house, and as André S. Labarthe has said: "The old mansion of the Ambersons is more than a dwelling; it is fixed to its inmates like the shell is to a snail."[95] It is the ideal repository for eavesdropping, gossip, and farewells. At the end, its furniture doomed with cloths, its rooms bereft of laughter and argument, it acts as a kind of confessional for George as he kneels by his mother's bed in contrition. For the spirit of the Ambersons lies as much in their household as in themselves, just as Kane's character is represented in Xanadu, and just as Arkadin's is in his Spanish castle.

George (Tim Holt) in earnest conversation with his mother Isabel (Dolores Costello).

THE MAGNIFICENT AMBERSONS

Scene: the hall of the Amberson mansion. George has just insulted Eugene Morgan about his respect for the new-fangled automobiles. His uncle Jack rebukes him and George dashes out of the dining room in a temper. Fanny, who has witnessed the scene, whispers to him. "George!" They walk towards the stairs: the camera follows them.

FANNY: You've struck just the right treatment to adopt . . . you're doing just the right thing.

GEORGE: Oh, what do you want?

FANNY: Your father would thank you, if he could see what you're doing.

GEORGE: You make me dizzy! Why the mysterious detective business?

FANNY: You don't care to hear that I approve of what you're doing?

GEORGE: For God's sakes, what in the world is wrong with you?

Fanny starts climbing the stairs, speaking with bitterness in her voice.

FANNY: Oh, you're always picking on me, always!

George follows her up the stairs. The camera moves with them as they ascend.

FANNY: —ever since you were a little boy!

GEORGE (*scornful*): Oh, my gosh!

FANNY: You wouldn't treat anybody in the world like this, except old Fanny! "Old Fanny," you say, "It's only old Fanny, so I'll kick her . . . nobody'll resent it. I'll kick her all I want to!" Then you're right. I haven't got anything in the world since my brother died. Nobody. Nothing!

GEORGE: Oh, my gosh!

FANNY: I never never in the world would have told you about it or even made the faintest reference to it . . .

She goes out of frame, still talking. George stops.

FANNY: . . . if I hadn't seen that somebody else had told you, or you'd have found out for yourself in some way.

GEORGE: Somebody else had told me what?

FANNY: How people are talking about your mother.

George climbs the stairs. The camera follows him to the balcony. He stops in front of Fanny, and speaks severely.

GEORGE: What did you say?

FANNY: Of course, I understood what you were doing when you started being rude to Eugene . . .

They move to the right. Close-up as Fanny speaks.

FANNY: I knew you'd give Lucy up in a minute if it came to a question of your mother's reputation.

GEORGE: Look here!

She stops, turns around, and watches George from above as they talk.

FANNY: . . . because you said . . .

GEORGE: Look here! Just what do you mean?

FANNY: I only wanted to say that I'm sorry for you, George, that's all . . .

Fanny turns and ascends to the right. George follows her. Close-up.

FANNY: . . . but it's only old Fanny, so whatever she says, pick on her

Fanny and George on the stairs.

for it. Hammer her! Hammer her!

GEORGE: Jack said . . .

They stop in front of the balustrade. Fanny talks hysterically. George stares at her angrily.

FANNY: It's only poor old lonely Fanny!

George is furious.

GEORGE: Jack said that if there was any gossip, it was about you! He said people might be laughing about the way you ran after Morgan, but that was all.

FANNY: Oh yes, it's always Fanny, ridiculous old Fanny . . . always . . . always!

GEORGE: Listen. You said mother let him come here just on your account, and now you say . . .

FANNY: He did. Anyhow, he liked to dance with me. He danced with me as much as he did with her . . .

GEORGE: You told me mother never saw him except when she was chaperoning you.

FANNY: Well, you don't suppose that stops people from talking, do you? They just thought I didn't count! "It's only Fanny Minafer," I suppose they'd say. Besides, everybody knew he'd been engaged to her.

GEORGE: What's that?

FANNY: Everybody knows it. Everybody in this town knows that Isabel never really cared for any other man in her life.

GEORGE: I believe I'm going crazy. You mean you lied when you told me there wasn't any talk?

FANNY: It never would have amounted to anything if Wilbur had lived.

GEORGE: You mean Morgan might have married you?

FANNY: No, because I don't know that I'd have accepted him.

Script Extract

THE MAGNIFICENT AMBERSONS

A key scene in which Lucy, whose father Eugene Morgan has become a famous designer of automobiles, reveals her nostalgia for the days when she was in love with the the vindictive Georgie Minafer.

The scene takes place in the garden. Medium shot, taken from below as Lucy and Eugene come from the background towards the camera. Eugene knocks his pipe against the palm of his hand. Lucy speaks while they come into focus. An orchestra plays GARDEN MUSIC.

LUCY: Ever hear the Indian name for that little grove of beech trees?

EUGENE: No . . . and you never did either. Well?

They stop. Lucy laughs.

LUCY: The name was Loma-Nashah. It means, "They-couldn't-help-it."

EUGENE: Doesn't sound like it.

LUCY: Indian names don't.

They come into the foreground. The camera retreats.

LUCY: There was a bad Indian chief, the worst Indian that ever lived, and his name was . . .

They stop again.

LUCY: . . . it was Vendonah. Means "Rides-down-everything."

EUGENE: What?

They face each other while talking.

LUCY: His name was Vendonah, same thing as "Rides-down-every-thing." *She laughs.*

EUGENE: I see. Go on.

LUCY: Vendonah was unspeakable. He was so proud he wore iron shoes and walked over people's faces. So at last the tribe decided that it wasn't a good enough excuse for him that he was young and inexperienced. He'd have to go. So they took him down to the river, put him in a canoe, and pushed him out from shore. The current carried him on down to the ocean. And he never got back. They didn't want to get him back of course. They hated Vendonah, but they weren't able to discover any other warrior they wanted to make chief in his place. They couldn't help feeling that way.

EUGENE: I see. So that's why they named the place, "They-couldn't-help-it."

LUCY: Must have been.

They come close up to the camera, which draws back. They stop.

EUGENE: So you're going to stay in your garden. You think it's better just to keep walking about among your flower beds and get old . . . like a pensive garden lady in a Victorian engraving? Huh?

LUCY: I suppose I'm like that tribe that lived here, papa, I had too much unpleasant excitement. I don't want any more. In fact, I don't want anything but you.

EUGENE: You don't. What was the name of that grove?

LUCY: "They-could . . ."

EUGENE: No, the Indian name, I mean.

LUCY: Oh . . . Mola-Haha.

They laugh together.

EUGENE: Mola-Haha . . . that wasn't the name you said.

LUCY: Oh, I've forgotten.

EUGENE: So you have. Perhaps you remember the chief's name better?

LUCY: I don't.

Eugene puts his arm around her, and says thoughtfully

EUGENE: I hope some day you can forget it.

They go out of frame.

THE STRANGER

"I believe, thinking about my films, that they are based not so much on pursuit as on a search. If we are looking for something, the labyrinth is the most favourable location for the search. I do not know why, but my films are all for the most part a physical search"—ORSON WELLES[29]

PLOT OUTLINE—Inspector Wilson of the Allied War Crimes Commission goes to Harper, Connecticut, in the hope of unmasking the notorious Nazi leader, Franz Kindler, now posing as a school master under the name of Charles Rankin. At the same time another ex-Nazi, named Meinike, arrives in Harper, deliberately set free by Wilson's Commission in the hope that he may lead them to Kindler, his old colleague. But Kindler strangles Meinike in a wood for fear of his identity being discovered. Wilson is certain of Rankin's real background when the latter lets fall at dinner one evening the remark, "[Karl] Marx wasn't a German, he was a Jew." Subsequent circumstantial evidence, combined with the unearthing of Meinike's body, enables Wilson to persuade Kindler's newly-wed wife of her husband's guilt. She is nearly killed by the maniacal Kindler, but Wilson intervenes and the Nazi falls to his death from the local clock tower.

IN EUROPE IN 1946, there was a strong tide of feeling running in Welles's favour; *Citizen Kane* reached Paris only after the war, and inspired a whole series of laudatory articles in intellectual film periodicals. The fact that Welles had enjoyed only partial control in the final shaping of *The Magnificent Ambersons* was overlooked; and few

84

Welles as Charles Rankin/Franz Kindler in THE STRANGER.

people at this stage knew the extent of the *débâcle* in South America
(which, oddly enough, was only to make headlines in European film
circles in 1970 when Charles Higham and Richard Wilson were disputing the facts of the matter).

These reverential tributes to a man who had played havoc with
Hollywood conventions were prompted mainly by the dazzling style
that Welles had acquired with the help of Gregg Toland. Few critics
at this stage bothered to discuss Welles's attitudes and themes. Besides,
Citizen Kane and *The Magnificent Ambersons,* differing from each
other in both time and sentiment, offered little clue in themselves to
the underlying ideas that were to obsess their maker in the next twenty-
five years.

The Stranger and *The Lady from Shanghai* then gave, in quick
succession, a number of indications of Welles's view of the world. Both
films are about the cancerous power of evil in (American) society.
Attempts on the part of Welles to define the limits and the strength
of justice may be discerned, and these are to become even more pronounced in *Touch of Evil* and *The Trial.* In both films, too, the leading figure—in *The Stranger,* Charles Rankin/Franz Kindler, and in
The Lady from Shanghai, Michael O'Hara—is a solitary, a wanderer
without a home, hovering on the edge of a society that cannot make up
its mind whether or not to accept him. Such figures, irrespective of
their material wealth or importance, can be pinpointed in a majority
of Welles's films: Kane, the great original; Georgie Minafer; Macbeth
and Othello, obviously; Arkadin (and even Van Stratten); Quinlan;
and Joseph K. Even so stereotyped a film as *The Stranger* fits the detective figure of Wilson into the Wellesian pattern—an instrument of
Nemesis who, like Iago, will not be silent until he has dragged down
his victim.

Welles in the late Forties was threshing ever more hopelessly in the
enveloping net of the Hollywood system. If he had not torn himself
free of it he might never have made another film (and he has little
praise now for the independent producers who gradually became more
powerful than the major studios themselves). He certainly would never
again have obtained the freedom granted him so glibly in 1940 by
RKO, or the control over the editing that he was to have with *Othello*
and *The Trial.*

He recalled recently: "I never expected to have control over the
editing of *The Stranger,* since Sam Spiegel was the producer. This is
the only picture I have made in which I did not at least expect to
function as a producer (in the American sense of the word). The best
stuff in the picture was a couple of reels taking place in South America.

Spiegel cut it out entirely. There was also a famous fight about a close-up. He wanted to cut into a scene for a close reaction of Loretta Young. I was opposed to this and, remarkably enough, Miss Young took my side in a heated debate involving Spiegel, her agent and a number of other officials. Because the female star demanded that she should *not* have a close-up, we won the day."† John Huston was by all accounts the real author of the script, although Welles also worked with Anthony Veiller on it, uncredited. Presumably the film was produced with the prime intention of making capital out of the immediate postwar fear of fifth columnists and Nazi infiltration in America itself. The figure of Franz Kindler may have been based on any one of several Nazi criminals, including Martin Bormann. Incidentally, the film clips of concentration camp atrocities shown to Kindler's wife and her father by Wilson must have been among the first ever revealed to the cinema-going public.

The narrative flow of the film is established in a remarkable opening reel, in which one sees the detective leaving his Commission for war crimes determined that, "This obscenity must be destroyed!" Like the ubiquitous reporter in *Citizen Kane,* he has a mission: not to solve the mystery of a famous man's dying words, but to bring a war criminal to justice, none less than Kindler who, according to Wilson, "conceived the theory of genocide" and had a passion for anonymity.

The scene then switches to a waterfront, and Russell Metty's camera stalks the figure of a man (Meinike, a Nazi concentration camp commander) as he hurries down gangways and corridors and across shadowy wharves. This sequence is the perfect visual description of an unseen enemy entering the citadel by night. Meinike, recently become a religious fanatic in an attempt to atone for his crimes, visits an unidentified South American country, his face sharply caught in the lens of a camera as he demands Kindler's address from the agent who is preparing his false passport.

Next, in the sleepy town of Harper, Welles uses an imaginative crane shot that comes down through the trees of the town square as the bus swings round by the church and Meinike alights, followed by Wilson. But the melodramatic touches that mar the entire film now proliferate. Meinike bursts unconvincingly into the Rankin household. The camera concentrates on Kindler's furtive, restless eyes and tremulous jaw as he meets his former accomplice in the woods, and commits ineffectual cranes as—having throttled the newcomer to Harper in the midst of a grotesque "confession"—Rankin is almost caught by some boys following a paper chase nearby. With unlikely aplomb, he returns immediately to wed Mary Longstreet, daughter of a Supreme Court

Inspector Wilson (Edward G. Robinson), with clock tower looming in the background.

Judge and then, even more implausibly, deserts the reception to bury Meinike's corpse.

The one subtly-written scene of the film takes place at a dinner party to celebrate the return of the honeymooners. There, the subject of Nazi resurgence is broached casually by Wilson (now posing as an antiques expert) and Rankin, waxing arrogant, launches into a disquisition on the German character, for whom "The Messiah is not a Prince of Peace—he's another Barbarossa, another Hitler," and makes his first error when he tells his young brother-in-law, Noah, that "Marx wasn't a German, he was a Jew." But this sinister mood is dispelled when Kindler illogically takes his dog out for a walk in the woods late at night, and the animal scrabbles away furiously at the spot where Meinike's corpse is buried. As the evidence builds up against him, Kindler's actions become even more absurd, his passion for clocks scarcely matching his presumed background of violence and sadism. Yet he is a true "scorpion" in the Wellesian sense. He is patently reluctant to kill his wife, even when she hands him a poker and asks

Wilson confronts Mary Longstreet (Loretta Young) and her father (Philip Merivale) with evidence of Kindler's crimes.

Wilson explains Mary's behaviour to her father.

him to do his worst. Instead he rushes back to the clock tower, to die in a private Götterdämmerung on high.

Another serious flaw in the script is the inhuman behaviour of the wife. Suspicious of him at the first hint of his false identity, she makes it seem unbelievable that she would, only a few days earlier, have given her life to Charles Rankin in marriage. The final sequence, as Mary and Wilson pursue the now unmasked Kindler to the top of the clock tower, is echoed three years later in the death of Harry Lime in the sewers of Vienna, and, like Lime, Kindler speaks contemptuously of his gazing down like God at the "little ants" searching the woods for him. The grotesque and gruesome end, with Kindler impaled on a sword-bearing effigy (a real *ange purificateur!*) revolving round the clock as it chimes the hour, is in keeping with nearly all Welles's other films; it represents the deserts of a villain, as does Quinlan's death in the slime of the river bank, or Iago's incarceration in the cage above the rocks, or the dramatic end of *Confidential Report* as Arkadin throws himself from his private plane.

At odd moments in *The Stranger,* Welles's talent emerges. He has admitted, "The only little things about it I really like are the comments

Small talk in the drugstore. Billy House and Edward G. Robinson.

Kindler draws his wife up to the belfry.

Potter (Billy House) dons a black cap as Rankin senses that his plans have gone awry.

Wilson intervenes as Kindler is about to shoot his wife.

The end for Kindler, about to be impaled.

on the town, the drugstore man, details of this kind."[40] It is true that
these scenes in the "do-it-yourself" drugstore, as Wilson (played su-
perbly throughout by Edward G. Robinson) passes his time in playing
checkers with the wry-spoken town clerk, are engaging and early in
the film make imaginative use of overlapping sound—raucous laughter
from Billy House, a radio commentator's voice, customers' conversation, and so on. Elsewhere the soundtrack is orthodox to a degree.
Welles conjures up a certain atmosphere in the Harper school gym
where Wilson searches for Meinike and is knocked cold with a pair of
rings, and the swimming pool waits, smooth and deserted; in the clock
tower, where one shot looks up at Rankin, sawing through the rung
of the ladder like a distant spider spinning in his web; and in the
Longstreet home, where Wilson projects Nazi film clips and stands
before the screen in the same way as Hastler does in *The Trial*.

Despite Welles's lack of control over the production, there are one
or two effective pieces of editing. As Rankin kicks the dog frantically
away from the shallow grave in the woods, the film cuts to Wilson,
starting up in bed, aroused not by any noise but by the revelation that
Rankin must be Kindler if he denies Marx's German nationality. But
for the most part the film is as uncomfortable an experience to watch as
it must have been for Welles himself to make.

THE LADY FROM SHANGHAI

"I know that in theory the word is secondary in cinema but the secret of my work is that everything is based on the word. I do not make silent films. I must begin with what the characters say. I must know what they say before seeing them do what they do"—ORSON WELLES[29]

PLOT OUTLINE—Michael O'Hara, an itinerant Irishman, is lured by the beautiful Elsa Bannister into joining the crew of her husband's yacht, after he has rescued her from some thugs in Central Park. Elsa's husband is a brilliant, but crippled lawyer. His sinister partner, Grisby, persuades the gullible O'Hara to accept five thousand dollars in exchange for framing a disappearance act decked out as murder. O'Hara finds that Grisby is killed in earnest and that he is the principal suspect. Bannister defends O'Hara in the trial, but the latter escapes before a verdict is returned only to discover, during a Chinese theatre performance in San Francisco, that Elsa is the real villainess and that her gun killed Grisby. He is taken by Elsa's accomplices to a deserted fairground, where Bannister and his wife shoot out their differences in a mirror maze. O'Hara leaves Elsa to die.

THE FILMING OF THE LADY FROM SHANGHAI was as exotic as its theme. Errol Flynn's yacht, the "Zaca," was chartered (with Flynn as skipper) for the scenes off the Mexican coast, and other exteriors were shot on the waterfront at Acapulco, then in Chinatown, San Francisco (the theatre scenes were filmed at the Mandarin Theatre), and in the Playland amusement park in the same city. The plot tended to become more cryptic as shooting progressed, there was an infinite

Welles shooting THE LADY FROM SHANGHAI on the waterfront in Acapulco. Rita Hayworth in the background.

number of post-production problems, and the film was a failure at the box-office. Yet somehow *The Lady from Shanghai* exudes a strong appeal for Welles enthusiasts, perhaps on account of its fantasy element.

Parts of the film are, like *The Stranger*, embarrassing, but as a whole it is far more successful; everything about it seems closer to Welles's heart—the theme, the imagery, the setting, the outcome. Yet one hesitates to agree with those French critics who speak of this film as a poem; indeed one hesitates to apply the term "poet" to Welles in any of his work. He is a superlative "prose" writer, without using the word in any pejorative sense. Those bravura effects in his *oeuvre* that presumably give rise to the word "poetic" are rather the equivalent of those passages in which a novelist such as Cervantes or Scott Fitzgerald suddenly heightens his style to the brink of the notorious purple passage.

"When I start out to make a fool of myself, there's little enough can stop me," says Michael O'Hara as he wanders along the road through Central Park one evening. Immediately, and with the clumsy fighting tactics he uses to dispatch the ruffians who attack the beautiful Elsa Bannister a few minutes later, O'Hara is revealed as a naïve, hapless wanderer; and he retains these characteristics to the very close of the film. Only his murder of a Franco spy in Spain in 1939 weighs on his conscience ("I killed a man once," he informs Elsa at their first meeting in the Park). This explains the courage he shows in accepting Grisby's bizarre proposal that in exchange for five thousand dollars he should take the blame for a murder that never happened. An adventurer of the same ilk as the Van Stratten of *Confidential Report,* he values his life only in so far as it yields him experiences, of however sordid or dangerous a nature.

Welles uses the dialogue as much as the imagery of the film to light up the contrasting facets of the story, alternately wry and sinister. When O'Hara takes the drunken Bannister back to his boat, he comments, "He was exactly as helpless as a sleeping rattlesnake"; and later,

The first sequence. Michael O'Hara (Orson Welles) meets "the lady from Shanghai" (Rita Hayworth) in Central Park.

O'Hara watches the drunken Bannister (Everett Sloane).

when the yacht (appropriately called "The Circe"), having passed through the Caribbean and the Panama Canal, reaches the Mexican coast, he relates the famous story of the sharks, while Bannister, Elsa and Grisby bicker among themselves during a lavish picnic. "Off the hump of Brazil I saw the ocean so darkened with blood it was black . . . till all about the sea was made of sharks and more sharks still. I got the first strike . . . then the beasts took to eating each other, in their frenzy they ate at themselves . . . you could smell the death reeking up out of the sea. . . . There wasn't one of them sharks in the whole crazy pack that survived."

Told in O'Hara's unhurried Irish brogue, the story, like the one about the frog and the scorpion that Arkadin tells his guests in *Confidential Report,* has an allegorical quality, and reflects the writhing machinations of the Bannisters and Grisby, each secretly striving to outwit and ruin the other, each feeding on the other's blood. The very fact that Bannister is a well-known lawyer brings the Law into greater disrepute; like Hastler in *The Trial,* Bannister is corrupt (note the way in which he greets the Pickwickian judge and the vicious District Attorney like old friends outside the courtroom). Just before the jury emerges, Bannister tells his victim, "I want you to live as long as pos-

Bannister and Elsa outside the court room.

O'Hara reads the "confession" prepared for him by Grisby (Glenn Anders).

sible before you die, Michael." Hardly an agreeable sentiment in a man who has just blandly described himself to his wife as, "the greatest living trial lawyer."

At a sweltering Acapulco, just before Grisby makes his weird proposition, O'Hara remarks, "Oh, there's a fair face to the land, surely, but you can't hide the hunger and the guilt. It's a bright, guilty world." These last two instincts, hunger and guilt, dominate not merely *The Lady from Shanghai* but also Welles's other films: a desperate craving for power on the one hand, and a resultant guilt complex on the other (*cf*. Arkadin, Kane, Quinlan, Clay). When eventually he gazes down at the dying Elsa, O'Hara murmurs, "Like the sharks, mad with their own blood, chewing away at their own selves." His forecast on the yacht has been fulfilled. His final words, as he strolls away from the deserted amusement park, revert to the engaging simplicity of the opening scenes: "Everybody is somebody's fool. . . . Maybe I'll live so long that I'll forget her. Maybe I'll die trying."

The imagery, too, richly counterpoints the theme of ambition and subterfuge. "On the yacht, the camera pivots, descends, withdraws, seeming to follow all the twisting thoughts of the characters."[82] Grisby's repulsive features are shown in monstrous close-ups, and as he ends his murder proposition to Michael with a glib, "So long, fella!" the camera looks down sharply at O'Hara at the end of the curved parapet above the bay of Acapulco, so that the Irishman seems suspended above a sheer void. One's sensation of vertigo is as powerful as O'Hara's fear of the scheme laid so diabolically before him. Charles Lawton's photography contributes to this visual unease. No reflectors were used during the Acapulco scene just described. "Welles was wearing a white linen suit which made his face look dark and sombre—while the lawyer wore grey clothes which did not contrast so sharply with his skin and made his complexion appear white and sickly."[100]

Then there is Bannister, with his protuberant eyes and a pair of crutches, who reminds one of Hank Quinlan and his lazy menace. Elsa begs O'Hara to elope with her from her predatory husband while, behind her, hideous conger eels, sharks, and even an octopus, slide slowly, slimily, beyond the glass of the Steinhardt Aquarium in San Francisco. In the Chinese theatre to which O'Hara flees to avoid the police after he has escaped from court, the players on stage, with their hieratic gestures and barbaric swordplay, provide a background that evokes the sacrifices and expiatory ceremonies not far removed from the primitive courtroom in which the verdict has only just been given.[40] There is a strikingly similar scene in Ingmar Bergman's *The Silence*, where a troupe of dwarfs cavort on the stage of a cabaret while Anna

The death of Broom (Ted de Corsia) as Elsa looks on.

watches a couple making love in the shadows. There is an erotic quality
to *The Lady from Shanghai* that is well mirrored in the romantic
sweep of the Caribbean and Mexican shorelines, the hot, eager beat
of the scenes in Acapulco, and then these unfamiliar sights and sounds
in San Francisco's aquarium and Chinatown. Only when this elaborate
superstructure is destroyed can the true outlines of the imbroglio
become clear.

So to the memorable final reel. O'Hara wakes up (as K wakes up
in *The Trial*) to find himself in an empty amusement park; by accident he trips off a machine in the "Crazy House" that sends him sliding
and rolling helplessly through a series of obstacles—Lawton and his
camera operator had to slide down a 125-foot chute to film this. With
its baroque shadows and heaving *décor,* this scene (only a fraction
remains in the finished film) epitomises the hero's mental and physical
instability in a distorted world. In the Hall of Mirrors to which he
finally finds himself drawn, huge close-ups mingle with fragmented
images. Bannister and Elsa confront each other and endless multiplica-
tions of their own likeness. The shooting is wild, and the smashed
mirrors suggest what Henri Agel has called a dislocation of physical
harmony.[53] Welles says that originally there was no music on the sound-

O'Hara is swept down the helter-skelter slide.

A brilliant composition from the gun fight in the mirror maze, as Bannister falls dying in the reflections.

track in this scene, just the ricochetting of bullets and crashing glass.* Several two-way mirrors were used to enable the camera team to shoot through them from the non-reflecting side.

Purely in technical terms, this sequence is a *tour de force,* preceded in time only by that early chase in *The Circus,* when Chaplin eludes a pursuing policeman in a mirror maze. But the climax has far wider connotations. It embodies the destruction of a myth, the myth of the good-hearted heroine in American films. "Each time a mirror falls in fragments, it carries with it the face of Rita. It is not only the body of the woman that perishes, but the idea, the allegory of Woman."[124] Rita Hayworth, Welles's second wife, had become enshrined in *Gilda* two years previously. Yet in *The Lady from Shanghai* Welles destroys the glamour surrounding her with a remarkable ease and subtlety. At every possible moment he shows her, sardonically, in the conventional, romantic light, and then, at the end, "He smashes the perfect shell of the ideal woman and the *femme fatale* is revealed."[124] At the beginning of the film Elsa is clearly marked as the damsel in distress, rescued by the cavalier adventurer, Michael O'Hara. On the yacht, the camera hovers over her admiringly as she sings one of those sentimental love songs that seemed the prerogative of any star with any kind of voice in the high Forties. Even Bessie, the yacht's cook, is deceived by Elsa. "That poor little babe he's married . . ." she says.

Then, as Grisby comes briefly aboard, his sticky malevolence seems to taint all but Elsa, as she sunbathes on a distant rock. She is not "the siren who attracts ships and destroys sailors with her charms, but Andromeda awaiting Perseus."[124] This continual isolation of Elsa as the beautiful female beyond reproach (her white dresses seem symbolically to bestow this purity upon her), dominated by a scheming husband and interested only in true love, is shattered in the Chinese theatre when O'Hara finds the gun that killed Grisby, in her handbag. One is already unnerved when she starts speaking Chinese to her contacts. It reveals in her an unexpected facility and self-possession. And when Michael leaves her in the Hall of Mirrors, he flies in the face of tradition; hitherto heroines, if they had died at all, had usually died in the arms of the hero. But Elsa, like Brigid O'Shaughnessy in *The Maltese Falcon,* is abandoned for the traitor she is.

Beyond this, however, there is a sense of inexorability about Elsa's conduct. Arkadin will tell the story of the frog and the scorpion to his party in *Confidential Report* as an implicit *apologia* for his pattern of behaviour. Here Elsa regales O'Hara with a Chinese proverb that concludes, "One who follows his nature keeps his original nature in the end." In the aftermath of battle in the mirror maze, O'Hara quotes the story back at the dying Elsa—"But haven't you heard of something better to follow?" The line suggests a higher morality not often referred to in Welles's work.

It would be wrong, though, to describe *The Lady from Shanghai* in purely tragic terms. The courtroom scene bubbles with a manic, unsettling humour, and acts in the manner of Shakespeare as a kind of respite before the violent climax. O'Hara's Irish mischievousness and blarney also lighten the tone, and at the same time contain the truth that can only later be discerned. "I don't like my girl friends to have husbands. If she can fool her husband I figure she can fool me," he says when he discovers that Elsa is married. There is black humour, too, particularly in the character of Bannister as so brilliantly created by Everett Sloane, both at the outset, when he is tempted into drunkenness by O'Hara and his mates, and at the very end when, about to die from his wife's pistol shots, he gasps, "You made a mistake, lover, you

"Give my love to the sunrise!" O'Hara abandons Elsa at the conclusion of THE LADY FROM SHANGHAI.

Court room tension and badinage: the District Attorney (Carl Frank) and Bannister appeal to the Judge while O'Hara (right) looks on.

should have let me live—you're going to need a good lawyer!"

The evil in *The Lady from Shanghai* lurks beneath the surface, and is all the more sordid and hideous when it emerges at the end. For much of the time, as in *The Trial*, everybody and yet nobody seems guilty. But in the Wellesian universe the wages of sin are death, and Elsa and her husband are doomed as surely as Hank Quinlan, Gregory Arkadin, and Franz Kindler.

MACBETH

"Film is a very personal thing, much more than theatre, because the film is a dead thing —a ribbon of celluloid—like the paper on which one writes a poem. Theatre is a collective experience; cinema is the work of one single person—the director"—ORSON WELLES[43]

PLOT OUTLINE—Macbeth and Banquo, generals of Duncan (King of Scotland), returning from a victorious campaign against rebels, come upon three witches (in the film, "The Three"). They prophesy that Macbeth shall be "thane of Cawdor" and then King, and that Banquo "shall beget Kings though he be none." News comes that the King has in fact made Macbeth thane of Cawdor. His ambition let loose, and spurred on by Lady Macbeth, he murders Duncan. Then, to offset the danger of Banquo's fulfilling the witches' prophecy, Macbeth contrives his [Banquo's] murder as well as that of his wife and child. Attacked by Malcolm and Macduff, Macbeth is killed. Shortly beforehand, Lady Macbeth has lost her reason and committed suicide. Malcolm is hailed King of Scotland.

WELLES HAS CALLED SHAKESPEARE "the staff of life," and since his teens he has played Shakespearian roles and produced Shakespearian plays at the slightest opportunity. Lear, Othello, Macbeth, Falstaff, Brutus, Claudius—all have been transformed by him into something surpassing the conventional figures evolved over the centuries. "You know, in the old classical French theatre, there were always actors who played Kings and those who did not: I am among those who play Kings."[25] Certainly. his stature (he is six feet three inches tall) and bearing, allied to one of the most powerful and

Welles with Richard Wilson on the set of MACBETH.

expressive voices of his generation, equip Welles for Shakespeare's more memorable roles, and he dominates his film versions of *Macbeth, Othello* and *Chimes at Midnight* with an ease and a grandeur all the more astonishing when one learns the awkward circumstances surrounding their creation.

By using these Elizabethan sources in three of his films, Welles enables one to discover the antecedents of so much of his contemporary work. In many respects he loves the same themes as Shakespeare loved—the fall of a mighty figure, the several facets of comradeship—but in neither *Macbeth* nor *Othello* has he shown strict reverence for the letter of the play. For *aficionados* of Shakespeare's verse, these two films may be unattractive. Yet, cinematically, they house immense barbaric power. If they appear melodramatic, it is due to Welles's firm belief that "Shakespeare never wrote a pure tragedy; he couldn't do it. He wrote melodramas which had tragic stature, but which were nonetheless all melodramatic stories."[25]

"My purpose in making *Macbeth*," Welles has said, "was not to make a great film—and this is unusual, because I think that every film director, even when he is making nonsense, should have as his purpose the making of a great film. I thought I was making what might be a good film, and what, if the 23-day shooting schedule came off, might encourage other film-makers to tackle difficult subjects at greater speeds."[17] The changes Welles made are fairly radical. At the end, for instance, there is a pitched battle that takes place off-stage in the play (although Kurosawa's widely-praised *Throne of Blood*, made many years later, also relies on the final battle for some of its most striking effects), and the witches become "The Three," and, armed with forked sticks, are a collective, almost abstract symbol of evil. Their "Fair is foul, and foul is fair," is a key phrase that might be equally well applied to other Wellesian characters, to Elsa Bannister, for example, or to Leni in *The Trial*. On a final, spe-cifically Wellesian note, they drag from the mud a hideous baby-figure, hacked apart by the sword of Macduff.

Macbeth himself "offers us the example of a character twitching, caught and shaken between Good and Evil."[40] Lady Macbeth pro-pels him towards disaster, as Iago destroys Othello, as Elsa tempts

Welles as Macbeth and Jeanette Nolan as Lady Macbeth.

Lady Macduff (Peggy Webber) and her son (Christopher Welles) about to be killed.

O'Hara, as Quinlan taunts Vargas. Welles is at pains to underline her sexual challenge. She appears first on her white fur bed, as sensual a figure as Elsa sunbathing on *The Circe.* "Unsex me here, and fill me from the crown to the toe top full of direst cruelty; . . . Come to my woman's breasts, and take my milk for gall," run her lines and, despite the inadequate range of Jeanette Nolan's performance, the erotic struggle and the "restless ecstasy" in Lady Macbeth's make-up are strongly communicated here. A disquieting touch is added by Welles, when Duncan is seen asleep in the same white fur bed just before his death. As Welles's version of the murder implies that Lady Macbeth stabs Duncan *before* her husband as well as after him, there is a faint, intriguing suggestion that she may have earlier seduced the King. Much later in the film, she whinnies like a frustrated mare in the grip of her "Out, damned spot!" speech, and urges her husband "to bed, to bed, to bed," although in the play Macbeth is not present in the scene.

Macbeth is already subconsciously disposed to evil. With his primitive outlook, he fears not the concept of murder, merely the sight of blood, the violence of the action itself. He is superstitious in his respect for the witches' spell even if he does, like all Shakespeare's tragic heroes, recognise his faults ("O! full of scorpions is my mind tonight"). His barbaric mind is reflected in the scenery (did not Welles once say that his characters are the best expression of the abject universe that has engendered them?). As he dons his square crown in a crudely formed mirror, his face stares back, tortured, distorted, and undulating ("To be thus is nothing"). The fear and insecurity that surround Macbeth are conveyed by Welles with a force that belies his pitifully small budget (around $200,000). The royal palace has no realistic form—its strength is abstract. In the distance, it rears above the clouds and vapours exactly as Xanadu does, remote and fantastic, at the start of *Citizen Kane*.

With their harsh shadows, their strange, writhing shapes, deformed

"Stonehenge-powerful, unrelieved tragedy." An execution in MAC-BETH.

windows, stairways, arches, and parapets, the sets are a latterday approximation to the conventions of the Elizabethan stage, where a tree painted on a placard represented an entire forest. Welles says that he wanted an atmosphere of sheer "Stonehenge-powerful, unrelieved tragedy."[99] The characters glance down on one another from strange slabs of rock. Beneath the castle there are caverns with walls that sweat like a guilty man; like, indeed, Macbeth when he is confronted by Banquo's ghost at the table and shadows coil over his terrified features. While the witches intone their off-screen warning that Birnam Woods will come to Dunsinane, Macbeth stands in a pool of light, staring up into the camera and the enveloping darkness. Welles's best effects are those that come and go before their artifice can be detected. There are, for example, some unearthly shots of the "woods" shifting suddenly through the mist and cloud above a ridge, with the sound of pipes skirling in the background.

As so often in Welles's work, light is seen as a purifying element. Macbeth and his wife hatch their plans in semi-darkness (her "Come, thick night," is given visible form); and there is an emphasis on the

MACBETH: a Holy Father (Alan Napier) falls dead with a spear in his chest.

Macbeth brooding on his throne (note the unusual crown).

blackness of the branches from which Macbeth's men unsaddle the
doomed Banquo. As Macbeth gasps, "Is this a dagger which I see
before me?" the images grow blurred, become suffused with gloom—
and so on. Only at the end, with Macbeth decapitated after a fierce
struggle on the battlements, does light assert its strength and honesty,
as hundreds of torches are brandished in acknowledgement of Scotland's new King, Malcolm. But the off-screen lighting, so effective later
in *The Trial,* is flagrantly anachronistic in this production, with steady
arcs where flickering light would be more convincing.

So, despite the poverty of the film's production values and the
unsettling rhythm of the dialogue (much of it spoken off-screen or
seeming to come from the "wrong" side of the camera), there are
things to praise in *Macbeth*—the outlandish quality of it all, the sur-
prising respect for Scottish accents, the raw authenticity of the costumes
(horns on Macbeth's helmet in the style of Ninth century Scottish
battle gear, armour consisting of circular plates of beaten metal, soldiers

MACBETH: the climactic fight on the battlements.

with plaited hair and squat iron nose shields), the intelligent use of extras, their lances and standards clustered closely to suggest might and menace, and the unerring sense of a man's psyche in the process of disintegration—a quality the film shares with *Othello*. The highest pitch of Macbeth's madness is reached in the dinner sequence. Macbeth stares down the long table in increasing fright, sensing the spirit of Banquo before gasping, "Which of you have done this?" But when Banquo and Duncan *do* reappear, each does so only for a second, and it is towards a mere hallucination that Macbeth stumbles so fearfully, overturning the table in the face of the camera, the lowslung ceiling of the chamber pressing down on him. All the timeless panic of Macbeth is contained in this moment.

OTHELLO

"In the theatre there are 1,500 cameras rolling at the same time—in the cinema there is only one"—ORSON WELLES[29]

PLOT OUTLINE—Desdemona, daughter of the Venetian senator, Brabantio, marries the Moor, Othello, in secret. Othello is informed on by his trusted ensign Iago (angered by Cassio's promotion to the lieutenancy), and is asked to explain his conduct before the Duke. Then he is called away in his capacity as a general of the Venetian state; Brabantio reluctantly allows him to take Desdemona with him to Cyprus. Iago soon instils in Othello's mind a terrible jealousy of Cassio, who is induced to flirt with innocent Desdemona. The Moor smothers his wife in her bed and finally, on discovering that he has killed her without genuine cause, stabs himself to death. In the film, Iago is placed in a cage and suspended from the castle while the funeral *cortège* of Othello, Desdemona, and Emilia (mortally wounded by Iago, her husband) winds its course.

ONE IS IMMEDIATELY PREPARED for the tone of Welles's *Othello* by the pre-credits sequence, which leaps right to the end of the play and lets the audience know the outcome of the tragedy. Welles does this also in *Citizen Kane* and *The Trial*, so that attention may be concentrated on *how* the plot is being unravelled, rather than on what it will lead to. A kind of iris-in—a parting of dark curtains—reveals the upturned face of the dead Othello as he is about to be carried to rest. The deep, resonant music, supported by a choir's singing a solemn dirge, accompanies the scene, as the funeral *cortège* proceeds slowly along the ramparts. The black, cowled figures against the skyline evoke *Electra* or *The Seventh Seal*, and the inert corpse of Othello calls to

Orson Welles as Othello.

mind Milton's "gorgeous Tragedy /In sceptred pall come sweeping by."

But the sudden appearance of Iago, dragged on a halter through the crowd to be imprisoned in a cage, is done in Welles's unique manner, ending with shots of the man gazing down at the people below with a mixture of fear and malevolence, while a winch hoists the cage inexorably upwards. Welles's vision of Iago's fate is typically savage: the punishment, as in *The Stranger* and *Touch of Evil,* is as cruel as the crime. And the cage reappears, pregnant with menace, at key points in the film, as a kind of reflection of Iago's evil—for instance when Iago muses, "So will I turn her virtue into pitch, /And out of her own goodness make the net /That shall enmesh them all."

Welles reads aloud an introductory text telling of Othello's eminence and secret love for Desdemona. This serves a similar purpose to the newsreel in *Citizen Kane,* in that it places one at once in the surroundings where the drama is to unfold. Welles in fact wastes very little time on niceties in any of his Shakespearian films. The montage is extremely fragmented (there are about five hundred shots in *Othello*) and dissolves are prolific. Lack of an adequate budget was a contributory cause of this style, but it suits Welles's purpose admirably in view of the fact that he has to pack so much into ninety minutes of running time. In the trailer for the film, Welles claims, "None of our settings were built in the studio. They are all real," as if conscious of the cheap studio fabrications of *Macbeth.* When the camera moves in *Othello,* it seems to weave a cocoon of intrigue around the characters. The film becomes an elaborate orchestration of jealousy and suspicion. There is only one really long take, which was shot from a jeep, as Othello and Iago walk along the battlements; this unbroken shot conveys splendidly Othello's mounting irritation and apprehension as his ancient echoes his words like a mocking-bird:

IAGO: I did not think he [Cassio] had been acquainted with her.
OTHELLO: O! Yes; and went between us very oft.
IAGO: Indeed!
OTHELLO: Indeed! Ay, indeed! discern'st thou aught in that?
    Is he not honest?
IAGO: Honest, my lord?
OTHELLO: Honest! Ay, honest.
IAGO: My lord, for aught I know.
OTHELLO: What dost thou think?
IAGO: Think, my lord!

Although Welles endows his Othello with nobility and compulsive power, Iago remains a more subtly-drawn character. Micheál MacLiam-

Othello and Iago in conversation. This long shot was taken from a slow-moving jeep.

móir, whose scintillating book[49] about the filming of *Othello* provides a rare insight into Welles's methods, gives Iago a lean and hungry look. He appears forever to be harbouring resentment, not merely against the Moor but against the world in general. A terrible loneliness exists within him as it does within Arkadin and Quinlan. Welles shows him lurking at the back of the church where Othello and Desdemona are married in stealth, whispering hoarsely to Roderigo, "I have told thee often, and I re-tell thee again and again, I *hate* the Moor!" Time after time the wind blows his hair about his face, making him look like some predatory animal; his headgear resembles a vulture's straggling hood. He slinks between the pillars of the castle and eyes Desdemona lasciviously. Welles shows him repeatedly in a superior position, forever gazing down on his victims from the battlements or a stairhead as if he held sway over them. He wears an extraordinary beard, no more than a thin line beneath his chin. It lends him a Satanic air, although Welles maintains, "I have taken from him the diabolical quality and made him more human. The motive for his actions is supplied by the implication of impotence." While the film

Iago and Cassio (Michael Lawrence) "tipple" as Cyprus celebrates.

Iago (Micheál MacLiammóir) urges Roderigo (Robert Coote) to kill Cassio.

never makes this clear, the final scene does go farther than usual in furnishing an unspoken justification for Iago. When Othello, bewildered with sorrow and rage, asks, "Will you, I pray, demand that demi-devil why he hath thus ensnar'd my soul and body!", Iago replies, in close-up, "Demand me nothing: what you know, you know." The guilt, in that moment, is somehow transferred to Othello himself. Like O'Hara, like Vargas, he has been infected by the malignancy of his adversary. Similarly, in *Macbeth,* there is the suggestion that Lady Macbeth senses her husband's preordained guilt.

Yet it is difficult to divorce the sin from the human being. In all his dealings, with the Senate, and with Desdemona, Othello has shown himself a noble person, capable of restraint and deep fidelity; it is the disease imparted to him by Iago that makes the man act like a demon. "Jealousy," claims Welles, "is detestable, not Othello. But insofar as he is so obsessed by jealousy as to become its personification—in that sense —Othello is detestable." Welles elevates Othello's character in the final sequence, his camera tracking the dying man back through the colonnades to the bed chamber where, in an act of penance or restoration almost, Othello lifts the body of Desdemona from the floor and sets it on the bed before wheeling to address his last speech to the horrified gathering above.

Welles's severe abridgement of the play has aroused much criticism. But each fresh viewing of the film strengthens one's opinion that Welles *does* display a remarkable respect for Shakespeare's text, while simultaneously adapting it for cinematic purposes. In the first place, he always films Othello with a stationary camera during the major speeches. One thinks of his apologia to the Senate, "Most potent, grave, and reverend signiors . . .", when the camera never leaves his face save for brief flashes to his audience and to Desdemona's anxious face as she listens; of his pitiful soliloquy, "Farewell the tranquil mind; farewell content! Farewell the plumed troop, and the big wars that make ambition virtue!" which will find its echo in *Chimes at Midnight;* and of that sombre farewell, "I pray you, in your letters, /When you shall these unlucky deeds relate, /Speak of me as I am," when the darkness gathers about his head and the voice of the dying man seems all but disembodied. Elsewhere, of course, Welles has changed matters. Pieces of the text are transposed. Cassio is killed outright whereas in the play he emerges on a chair to testify his innocence to Othello, and Iago's long speeches have been more than trimmed. Nonetheless, the lover of cinema is recompensed with other delights: the music, with its thunderous piano chords that lend a barbaric splendour to the opening and closing scenes; and the North African locations, exploited

Othello about to stifle Desdemona (Suzanne Cloutier).

Othello looks round furtively as he kills Desdemona.

to the full (no stage version of the play could equal that turbulent scene when the waves crash and roar beneath the castle while all eyes look for a sail and the safe return of Othello).

The style is rich in imaginative devices. When the drunken Cassio pursues Montano through the castle vaults, he flounders in water, and the smoke from a score of torches eddies above the scene, as more and more soldiers clatter into sight and individual faces are lost in the hullabaloo. As Othello, tormented by his ensign's needling, gasps, "I'll tear her all to pieces!" the sudden boom of the surf on the castle walls counterpoints the wrath and force of his exclamation. Not long afterwards, while Othello eavesdrops on the rigged conversation between Iago and Cassio, the sound of squawking seagulls divides and mocks the phrases. When the Moor cries out, "O! Iago, the pity of it, Iago! . . . I will chop her into messes. Cuckold me!" Welles cuts to cannon after cannon firing to announce the arrival of Lodovico's ship. The resonance is similar to those trumpets that blast away while Hotspur girds up his loins for battle in *Chimes at Midnight*. And as Othello soliloquises on the battlements and ends, "Othello's occupation's gone," Welles shows a ship's sail being slowly and laboriously hauled down its mast.

In one of the most irresponsible articles ever written by a critic, William S. Pechter asserted that in *Othello*, "All is sacrificed to the *mise-en-scène,* but is a *mise-en-scène* now become an orgy of tilted camera angles, intricate composition, and florid chiaroscuro. Concern is now exclusively for effects, not effects directed toward the end of any total meaning but rather isolated effects, singular flashes of brilliance (and some, admittedly, brilliant), indulged in only for themselves. Each scene is invested with an impact out of all proportion to its meaning or its relevance to context; each scene played and shot as though it were climactic."[115] Oddly enough, *Othello* is the one Shakespearian play that bristles with climaxes, and Welles resorts to even fewer than the Soviet director, Yutkevich, in his colour version of *Othello* (1957). Besides, so many of these "effects" *are* contributory to a "total meaning." Take, for example, the scene in which Othello gazes into a circular mirror while Iago pours his venomous remarks into his ears—the mirror distorts Othello's image, precisely reflecting the imbalance of his mind, the unreason that Iago's influence is begetting. Or the quiet, meticulous way in which Iago removes his

OTHELLO: the circular mirror "precisely reflecting the imbalance of his mind."

master's armour while perjuring Cassio, seeming thus to strip away the Moor's resistance to his cunning. Or the conversations between Roderigo and Iago; when Iago holds Roderigo's white poodle in his arms it symbolises his power over this worthless prattler. The significance of bars is also skilfully stressed throughout the film: the diagonal bars of the window of Desdemona's bedroom, the bars of the immense gate that divides Othello from his troop at the end, the bars of Iago's cage— all suggest the idea of the net in which Iago dreams of enmeshing everyone. Yutkevich was to convert this wish into visual terms by having his Othello walk among an array of nets on the seashore; Welles's counterpart is a kind of latticework that covers the animals kept at the castle and that presses with its shape and shadows on Othello and Iago as they walk beneath it. Roderigo is caught similarly in a "cage" when he is stabbed by the sadistic Iago "in the manner of fish-catching in tropical waters."[49] as he cringes beneath the slatted boards of a Turkish bath. Even in this admittedly rather contrived scene, the bubbling, seething baths are a brilliant reminder of that "cistern for foul toads to knot and gender in," that Shakespeare speaks of through Othello's mouth.

Far from being attenuated, the play reveals under Welles's direction that restless, brooding aspect that lies hidden in the folds of Shakespeare's verse. The violent pace of the film, the voices that echo and ricochet off the walls and linger menacingly in the air, the urgency of the bells; all this helps to add verisimilitude to Othello's cry of, "Arise, black vengeance, from the hollow hell!" In the early stages of the film the Moor is seen in clear light, but as jealousy begins to undermine him, the shadows multiply until when he creeps towards Desdemona's bed chamber, saying softly to himself, "It is the cause, it is the cause, my soul," he is no more than a grotesque silhouette on the wall. Dreams defeated once again by darkness in the Wellesian universe. Othello's features appear sculpted in the gloom as he accuses Desdemona more and more violently.

The murder itself, with the silk sheet drawn tightly over Desdemona's features, makes a mockery of the girl's beauty and yet affords a perfect physical image of Truth's being extinguished. Welles dissolves to a long shot of Othello's tower, the cage dangling by its side, but this time no small square of lighted window is there to challenge its foreboding presence. And the image that crystallizes the cruelty of Welles's film is of Othello lying in a swoon after listening to Iago's accusations against his wife, his eyes cast up in terror at the gulls wheeling in the summer sky, his mouth dragged open—frozen in a silent scream of agony.

Immaculate composition: Desdemona prays while Othello talks with Emilia (Fay Compton).

Iago and Othello on the battlements.

CONFIDENTIAL REPORT/MR. ARKADIN

> "Look, there are two kinds of people in the world; those who give and those who ask, those who don't care to give and those who don't dare to ask"—ARKADIN, in the novel, *Mr. Arkadin,* by Orson Welles[4]

PLOT OUTLINE—A young American, Van Stratten, is engaged in cigarette smuggling when a man named Bracco, knifed in the back on the wharves of Naples, with his last breath whispers two names—Gregory Arkadin and Sophie—into the ears of his (Van Stratten's) girl friend, Mily. The American, believing the names to be the key to a fortune, tracks down Arkadin in his Spanish castle and strikes up a friendship with his daughter Raina, to whom the wealthy financier is devoted. At a party Arkadin claims that he cannot recall his life prior to 1927 and he commissions Van Stratten to prepare a report on his early career. Van Stratten accepts and learns from a series of bizarre characters (a tailor in Zürich, a flea-trainer in Copenhagen, a fence living as an antique dealer in Amsterdam, and a Polish baroness) that Arkadin began as a white slave peddler under the tutelage of Sophie. Sophie herself is now in Mexico and tells Van Stratten she bears no ill feelings towards Arkadin for the past. Then both Sophie and Mily are murdered—it transpires by Arkadin's henchmen. Van Stratten realises that Arkadin has used him as a catspaw to find out if he is in danger of blackmail by his former associates. But, on hearing that nothing can prevent his beloved daughter from learning the truth, Arkadin commits suicide by jumping from his private plane.

Orson Welles as Gregory Arkadin in CONFIDENTIAL REPORT.

CONFIDENTIAL REPORT (released as *Mr. Arkadin* in the U.S.) was adapted by Welles himself from a novel he had written for publication in France two years previously—although the basic idea for the film had preoccupied him from an even earlier point. It is a good book, and has a logical progression about it compared with the film, which is just about the most slovenly-edited of all Welles's works; one wonders who perpetrated such a travesty.

Welles sets his scene beautifully in the book and this is reproduced carefully in the second sequence of the film (which, rather foolishly, opens with one of the final episodes in the novel, thus giving an excessively parenthetical effect to the remainder of the film). A cripple murders Bracco on the quays of Naples harbour. Welles's verbal description is memorable: "He was hurrying clumsily along beside the white wall of the customs house. The lights along the waterfront cast his shadow, long, crooked and enormous, before him. He vanished behind the massive outline of a watercart which was moving slowly into a shed. The guards were blowing their whistles furiously, sharp noises uselessly piercing the nocturnal fog. The only echo was the stupid, impotent booming of the foghorn."[4] Yet, because of the irritating structure of the film in its released form, *Confidential Report* is important only for isolated scenes and for the overall conception of Arkadin, a figure so powerful that he would survive the worst butchering a film company's editing staff could conceive.

Gregory Arkadin is a remarkable amalgam of Wellesian heroes. Monstrous, odious, vicious, sly, egotistical—all these adjectives can be applied to him. Welles himself has observed: "Arkadin is closer to Harry Lime than to Kane, because he is a profiteer, an opportunist, a man who lives on the decay of the world, a parasite who nourishes himself on the corruption of the universe, but he doesn't try to justify himself, like Harry Lime, by considering himself a sort of 'superman.' "[25] But not even the sympathy for him that Welles's subtle playing arouses can separate Arkadin from the other scorpions—Kane, Georgie Minafer, Franz Kindler/Charles Rankin, Elsa Bannister and her husband, Iago, Quinlan, Hastler, Clay.

The significance of the word "scorpion" in Welles's world is made clear in this film. At the party in the castle, Arkadin tells some of his guests a fable. A scorpion, who could not swim, approached the bank of a stream and begged a frog there to carry him on his back to the other side. The frog complained that the scorpion would sting him. But the scorpion replied that this was impossible because he himself would then drown with the frog. So the pair set out across the stream. Halfway over the frog felt a piercing pain in his back. The scorpion had stung him. "Is that logic?" he cried, "No, it's not," answered the scorpion as they submerged together, "but I can't help it. It's my character," It is in Arkadin's "instinct" to "sting" those around him, because he *must* remain faithful to his nature. Welles says that "the point of the story is to show that a man who declares himself in the face of the world, I am as I am, take it or leave it, that this man has a sort of tragic dignity. It is a question of dignity, of verve, of courage, but doesn't justify him . . . Arkadin created himself in a corrupted world; he doesn't try to better that world, he is a prisoner of it."[43]

As with Kane, there has been considerable speculation as to the model for Arkadin in Welles's mind. Was it Lowenstein, the magnate who disappeared, also in an aeroplane, over the English Channel? Or Krueger? Or Zaharoff? In physical appearance Arkadin resembles no one. "All the world knew his huge bulk, his square-cut beard, his bristly hair, his vast furcoats, his great broad-brimmed hats, all the accessories which seemed specially chosen to emphasise, weighten and widen his massive figure."[4] In manner he is sinister and withdrawn,

"All the world knew . . . his square-cut beard . . . his great broad-brimmed hats . . ." Arkadin with Van Stratten (Robert Arden).

as if contemplating the void of loneliness that encompasses him; he
has the ability, in common with Kane, to charm people momentarily
with his velvet speech and anecdotes. But he lacks the overweening
self-confidence of Kane. He seems almost aware of the ludicrous
figure he cuts at times of crisis. In spirit, Arkadin is afflicted with
what might almost amount to an inferiority complex about his own
villainy, and he is desperate to prevent his daughter Raina from
ascertaining the truth about his background. Yet the way in which
he bellows with hysterical anguish across the airport crowds at the
end, offering ten thousand dollars for a ticket on the plane that is
speeding the news of his past to his daughter, has a compelling
majesty to it, like Richard III's plea for a horse on the field of
Bosworth. His entire life has been enclosed in a web of illusory
power, ever since that freezing day in 1927 when, forsaking his real
name of Wasaw Athabadze, he began his climb to grandeur. His
castle at San Tirso in Spain is described in the novel as "a real fairy-
tale castle, with turrets and a winding road and ramparts draped in
ivy."[4] At the ball he holds in memory of the local saint, the guests
wear Goya-esque masks that hide their true identity. He loves to use
the telephone, so as to disembody his commands and threats. And
although he pays Van Stratten handsomely for bringing his past to
light, his genuine desire thereby is to smother that past forever, so
that Gregory Arkadin will be recognised as a man whose wealth and
strength were virtually bestowed on him by divine decree. "Men
should be what they seem," as Iago tells Othello.

Van Stratten, rather uncomfortably played by Robert Arden, is
purely an instrument in the hands of Arkadin, like Leland and
Bernstein in *Citizen Kane* and O'Hara in *The Lady from Shanghai*.
Raina loses the impact she has in the original book ("Raina Arkadin
was proud, prickly, stubborn and distrustful"[4]), and it is the gallery
of minor personalities that Welles brings so engagingly to life on
the screen. Burgomil Trebitsch, the Amsterdam antique dealer who,
with his whining voice and eagerness to sell, reminds one of Titorelli
in *The Trial*; the drunken Oskar, reeling about on a lurching ship;
Sophie, chill and precise, more intent on her cards than on the ques-
tioning of Van Stratten; the grimy Jacob Zouk, alone in his attic
with its portrait of Hitler (upside down) and with a craving for goose
liver that leads to his death; and the Professor in Copenhagen who
is proprietor of "The Greatest Flea Circus on Earth," and can make
his pet creatures obey his orders with a delicate flick of the finger.
Correspondingly, the characters whom Welles creates are jerked
about by some unseen power, lurking possibly in lust, money, or

Michael Redgrave as Burgomil Trebitsch, in CONFIDENTIAL REPORT.

Van Stratten bargains with Jacob Zouk (Akim Tamiroff).

Mischa Auer as the Professor inspecting his fleas in CONFIDENTIAL REPORT.

Paola Mori as Raina with Van Stratten. Arkadin's castle looms in the background.

in a mere tendency to be fascinated by the grotesque or the exotic in life.

The *décor* and camera movements heighten this sense of the bizarre throughout *Confidential Report*. When Van Stratten tries to bargain with Trebitsch, the camera—set at a low angle—follows them in sinuous movements, in keeping with the style of the transaction to which the two characters abandon themselves.[52] During a love scene between Raina and Van Stratten, Welles employs deep-focus photography to show Arkadin looming behind them, as though the happiness of the pair was overshadowed in advance. On the Saint's Day in the town near Arkadin's castle, a procession of penitents marches through the streets to the accompaniment of a tolling bell (one thinks of the Cyprus bell in *Othello*—and had Bergman seen this film by chance before shooting the flagellants' scene in *The Seventh Seal?*). Their black robes are shadowed against the walls of the houses, and the event assumes a kind of malign significance. The baroque is prominent in the settings, not just at Arkadin's ball, but also in the climactic sequences in Munich, where Arkadin, sly-footed, pursues Van Stratten into a lofty Byzantinian church, and moulds into the congregation as if he were a medieval patriarch. The various themes of the music—flamenco, organillo, staccato—match the barbaric atmosphere of several scenes, while the famous German Christmas carol, "O Tannenbaum," overlays the snowy vistas with a gentle irony.

Confidential Report as a story—though not so much as a film—resolves itself into an unconscious quest for identity on the part of Arkadin. Originally, the credits were to have been superimposed over a cluster of bats wheeling in the darkness; the effect would have been to underline the idea of characters plunging about without rhyme or reason, in a desperate search for orientation. But this, like the simplicity of the novel itself (even if Welles dislikes the English translation), has disappeared and one can judge only the finished film. It is a great pity that *Confidential Report* should be of all Orson Welles's films at once the one truly original work and—in the end—the furthest removed from his intentions as a director.

TOUCH OF EVIL

> "A policeman's job is only easy in a police state Captain. . . . Who's the boss, the cop or the law?"—Mike Vargas in *Touch of Evil*

PLOT OUTLINE—Mike Vargas, narcotics investigator for the Mexican Ministry of Justice, is honeymooning in the frontier town of Los Robles when the millionaire Linnekar is killed by a time-bomb planted just as he crosses the border into the United States. The local police captain, Hank Quinlan, agrees truculently to co-operate with Vargas on the case. Joe Grandi, an underworld figure who owns the lonely motel at which Vargas's wife, Susan, is staying, is keen to ruin the Mexican's reputation, because he (Vargas) has nabbed his brother (the real gang boss) on a narcotics charge. Unexpectedly, Quinlan helps Grandi to kidnap Susan because he is enraged at having been caught by Vargas while planting dynamite on Linnekar's potential son-in-law, Sanchez. Vargas discovers further that Quinlan has falsified evidence throughout his remarkable career. Quinlan meanwhile murders Grandi, arranging the scene so that the drugged Susan seems to be responsible. Then Vargas manages to sway Quinlan's old associate, Menzies, to his side, and the latter contrives to record Quinlan's drunken confessions on a tape recorder. Quinlan discovers this, shoots Menzies, and is in his turn shot by his dying accomplice. As he dies, news arrives that Sanchez has in fact confessed, vindicating Quinlan's intuition but not his methods.

TOUCH OF EVIL marked a brief return to America for Welles in the late Fifties, and the film was shot mostly on location at Venice, California, an old coastal town about fifteen miles from Hollywood. At first he was only asked to act in the picture. He refused. Then

Welles and Janet Leigh on the set of TOUCH OF EVIL.

the producers approached Charlton Heston, who agreed to appear only if Welles would direct. And so Welles accepted the project—with two and a half weeks to go before production was due to start. "When I make this sort of picture," he has said, "for which I can pretend no special aptitude or interest—it is not 'for the money' (I support myself as an actor) but because of the greedy need to exercise, in some way, the function of my choice. I have to accept whatever comes along from time to time or accept the alternative of not working at all."[12]

All Welles's leading figures are lonely in themselves, often nursing some secret grudge against society and turning to immoral methods to gain the power they feel to be their due. Like the principals of classical tragedy, they are doomed to nemesis. But Welles has never deserted the contemporary world and its problems although he casts his films in a tragic mould. Justice is an ideal that he pursues, without success, in *The Lady from Shanghai, Touch of Evil,* and *The Trial.* "I firmly believe that in the modern world," he says, "we have to choose between the morality of the law and the morality of basic justice. That is to say between lynching someone and letting him go free. I prefer

Hank Quinlan (Orson Welles) and Susan (Janet Leigh) in TOUCH OF EVIL.

to let a murderer go free than to let the police arrest him by mistake."[43] Welles's belief clarifies many points in *Touch of Evil* (and, of course, in *The Trial*). The Hank Quinlan whom he portrays so convincingly is a policeman who will do anything to "crack the case" and to add to his string of successful arrests. So, when an American millionaire is blown up by a time-bomb on the Mexican border, Quinlan immediately arranges to frame the lover of the dead man's daughter, by planting two sticks of dynamite in his apartment. The fact that in the final seconds of the film this Sanchez apparently confesses to the crime matters little to Welles; the means, if not the end, are wrong. "He's wrong despite everything," asserts the director.

The Mexican investigator, Vargas, is Welles's mouthpiece throughout the film, much as Michael O'Hara is in *The Lady from Shanghai*. He has his suspicions about Quinlan from the start. "What makes you so sure it was dynamite?" he asks warily. One can sense the conflict beginning between these two men, just as one can between O'Hara and Bannister (who, significantly, moves like Quinlan in the manner of some loathsome reptile). Welles rounds off this opening sequence with Vargas's smiling, "Captain, you won't have any trouble from me!" and Quinlan's reply, loaded with menace, "You bet your sweet life I won't."

Vargas (Charlton Heston) with his wife in TOUCH OF EVIL.

Each man uses a person close to the other as a weapon. Quinlan arranges for Grandi, one of a family that rules Los Robles, to incriminate Vargas's wife as a dope addict; and Vargas eventually persuades Quinlan's lifelong henchman, Pete Menzies, to destroy his master by concealing a microphone under his coat and luring him into a confession of his illegal manoeuvres. Each man is shown to be sensitive and sentimental beneath a rugged exterior. It transpires that Quinlan's fanatical, ruthless approach to his job dates back to the day in 1917 when his wife was strangled (by "that half-breed, of course [Grandi]") and the killer escaped forever. Like Arkadin and even Kane, he is a slave to a past he cannot forget and only when Grandi has been throttled does the debt to the past appear to have been paid. Vargas ostensibly neglects his newly-wed wife while the investigation into Linnekar's death gets under way, but he loses all control when he learns that Susan has been drugged and framed by Quinlan; he wrecks Grandi's bar and beats up his nephews. And, finally, he resorts to underhand tactics himself to bring down his adversary. As Gilles Jacob has suggested, "Vargas is tainted by his contact with Quinlan . . . he has been stung, as it were, by the scorpion on his back [a reference to *Confidential Report*]."[91] This theme of the duel to the death runs like a fugue through all Welles's work. It is similar—to take an analogy dear to his heart—to the *corrida*.

Quinlan is, visually, the most memorable Wellesian character. With his vast paunch, his limp, wide-brimmed hat, his fancy for cigars and candy bars, his half-closed eyes, he resembles a monstrous toad whose touch and presence besmirch everything about it. Yet the curiously disgruntled look on his ill-shaven face provides a glimpse of the human being beneath the corruption. When he visits the aging prostitute Tanya in her bordello, the sound of the player piano arouses memories of some vanished past, and his expression assumes a wistful, almost childlike radiance. He loses his words in his throat. "Almost all serious stories in the world are stories of a failure with a death in it," says Welles. "But there is more lost paradise in them than defeat. To me that's the central theme in Western culture, the lost paradise."[28]

Quinlan sees Tanya twice, once at the beginning and once at the end of the film. On both occasions there is a moment of genuine simplicity that recalls other meetings in Welles's world—between Kane and Susan Alexander on that wet evening outside 185 West Seventy-fourth Street, between Van Stratten and Sophie, between Joseph K and Block. . . . When Quinlan asks her to foretell his future from her cards, Tanya replies steadily: "Your future is all used up," and suddenly through his besotted mind flits an inkling of his fate, almost as

Quinlan with Zsa Zsa Gabor in TOUCH OF EVIL.

if Quinlan had consciously decided to abdicate by entering this stretch of Grandi territory, to drop his guard and accept whatever the Fates have in store for him now that his wife has been avenged. It is the moment of truth that always comes to Welles's heroes just before their end. Unlike Kane, Quinlan's ruthlessness has not stemmed from material ambitions. As he says to Menzies in the final sequence, "I could have been rich . . . after thirty years . . . all I've got's a turkey farm." For Quinlan, power over money is secondary to power over people.

As he lies dying in the turgid river, Quinlan hears Schwartz, the D.A.'s assistant, turn to Tanya and say, "That was a great detective all right." "And a lousy cop," she answers. "Is that all you have to say for him?" asks Schwartz. "He was some kind of a man . . . what does it matter what you say about people?" comes the reply. The bald defence of Tanya's final remark recalls de Sade's dictum: "In a criminal society, one must be a criminal."[40] Quinlan, like Arkadin or Iago, distorts reality because he believes that beyond its superficial appearance reality conforms to his notions. Sanchez is guilty because Quinlan wills him so; as Jean Domarchi has pointed out,[79] if Lady Macbeth can suggest to her husband the idea of a murder, it is because she knows that Macbeth is *already* a murderer. The irony of *Touch of Evil* is that Quinlan is shot finally by his faithful accomplice. As he dies he mumbles how this is the second time he has stopped a bullet for Menzies (the first being when he had saved his life some time before—hence his limp). "Quinlan is the god of Menzies. And, because Menzies worships him, the real theme of the scenario is treason, the terrible impulsion that Menzies has to betray his friend."[25] His first pangs of conscience come in the records room, as Vargas uncovers the trials so skilfully and ruthlessly rigged by Quinlan; and misgivings develop into conviction when he finds the police chief's cane in the room where Grandi has been stran-

Welles selects a penetrating camera angle in TOUCH OF EVIL.

gled. Unwillingly he allows himself to deceive his master, and Henri Agel has aptly compared the hand Menzies has in Quinlan's death with the shooting of Harry Lime by his friend Holly Martins.[53]

If Quinlan and Vargas dominate the stage in *Touch of Evil,* the film would hardly be the convincing, disturbing thriller it is without those minor characters whom Welles, like Pieter Bruegel, always manages to place in the background of his work. The slavish Grandi, with his wig and unlit cigars, given to petty harangues and moments of malevolent humour, dancing around Quinlan's shuffling bulk like some fish around a barracuda; the various nephews and nieces who comprise his brother's gang, terrorising Susan in the isolated motel or tracking Vargas through the streets; and Menzies, the Sergeant, whom Quinlan calls "pardner" with more than mere familiarity, watching with ashen face the piecing together of Quinlan's corruption in the records room. Then there is the sinister blind woman in the shop where Vargas telephones his wife; one has the impression she is absorbing all the gentle love phrases he whispers to Susan, and is twisting them foully in her mind. And, perhaps drollest of all, the receptionist at the Mirador motel: nervous, beetle-like, eyes expanding in panic behind the spectacles, mumbling incoherently, he calls to mind the

Susan Vargas in her motel room with the "night man" (Dennis Weaver).

stunted clowns of the Shakespearian theatre, whose very ridiculousness supplies a sharp comment on the action. "He seems to crystallise the chaos . . . like the drunken groom in *Miss Julie* . . . a kind of powerless chorus that reflects to the maximum the tragic insecurity of this night."[53] The role was completely improvised.

But, as always, it is not only the characters and their actions that convey the full impact of a film by Orson Welles. *Touch of Evil,* although apparently edited behind its director's back (with a series of comedy sequences omitted), is much less disjointed than *Confidential Report,* and shows Welles's imagination at its most breathtaking. The opening shot, lasting well over three minutes, must have been incredibly difficult to set up. "It took us all night to get it," recalls Janet Leigh.[98] It starts with a close-up of a time-bomb being set and then, as Henry Mancini's tense, low-pitched score tock-tock-tocks on the soundtrack, the camera cranes up sharply to show the bomb being planted in the boot of Linnekar's car. Almost immediately the unsuspecting millionaire and his floosie emerge from the background and drive out through the streets towards the border. The camera travels back, on a high crane, in front of the car, and descends gently as Vargas and his wife cross the road at some traffic lights while Linnekar is held up. Welles then tracks alongside and in front of the couple as they stroll towards the control post, and cranes up again as Linnekar eases his car alongside them and halts for the formalities. A few words pass between Vargas and the customs official about the Grandi brother whom Vargas has just sent for trial, and then the camera moves beside the Mexican and his wife as they walk over the border. Suddenly, there is a blinding explosion as the time-bomb goes off, and Welles completes the shot with a close-up of the blazing car followed by a short zoom into the wreck. These three minutes are made suspenseful by the presence of the bomb, of which only the audience is aware, and at the same time the uninterrupted fluidity of the shot suggests the peace that is to be so rudely disturbed when the millionaire is killed. The effect is rather blunted in the finished film, because the producers insisted on superimposing the credits on the left of the screen, thus diverting one's attention from the action and, conversely, preventing one from absorbing the credits themselves. Originally, they were to have appeared as Tanya walks away across the bridge at the end.

There are several other long takes, but none compares in virtuosity with this initial shot. Often unnoticed are two four to five minute takes in Sanchez's apartment that must have been extremely tricky to film because of the presence of anything up to eight actors in a ceilinged set. Yet had Welles adhered to convention and broken up these scenes

The opening sequence of TOUCH OF EVIL. Above, Vargas and his wife talk to a border official across Linnekar and his floosie. Below, Ray Collins and Joseph Cotten look at the wreckage after the explosion.

Joanna Moore as Marcia Linnekar is led by Pete Menzies (Joseph Calleia) through the blazing remains of her father's car.

into fragments, they would have lost irremediably in both tension and claustrophobia. Again and again throughout his career Welles has demonstrated that the long take, as opposed to the syncopated montage of Eisenstein, allows the audience to immerse itself in the action happening on the screen.

In *Touch of Evil* Welles was for the first time able to rely principally on the 18.5mm lens. This is ideal for the scenes such as that in which Vargas is trailed by Grandi's nephews and strides towards the camera at right of frame, while the youths follow silently in the distance; or when Menzies finds Vargas in the long, high-walled records room and walks uneasily back and forth. The wide angle provides a vision greater in range than the human eye, which can focus on only one particular point at a time; in *Touch of Evil* it foreshortens and elongates perspectives by turns, thus mirroring the contortions of the action itself. Welles uses close-ups sparingly in this film, and when they do appear they fulfil a clear purpose, such as the close-up of Quinlan while—sinking fast—he listens to his confession being played back on the tape recorder, or of the black glove that he draws on before throttling Grandi (significantly, the glove in the foreground blots out

the face of its terrified victim in the background). This entire scene
of Grandi's death is, in fact, one of the very few in the film that was
untouched by the producers. It takes place in the hotel room of Susan
Vargas as she lies drugged on the bed. Quinlan asks Grandi to put out
the light; he does so, and the only illumination comes from the neon
sign that flashes on and off outside the hotel with inexorable regularity.
Then Quinlan dons his black gloves and, drawing a gun on Grandi,
tells him to telephone Menzies at police headquarters. After a brief
conversation he hangs up, locks the door of the bedroom and then
advances like a human steamroller on the bivering Grandi, who tries
desperately to attract attention by smashing the window above the
door. But Quinlan drags him savagely down and strangles him just
as his own wife had been strangled forty years earlier. The brightening
and fading of the reflected light on the action provides a similarly
scarifying effect to the swinging lamp in the store-room where Joseph K
sees the police officers being whipped in *The Trial*.

As in *The Trial*, too, the last scene is among the most powerful of
all. Menzies walks with the inebriated Quinlan across a landscape as
weird as any conceived by Kafka: spidery derricks pierce the night sky,
oil pumps rise and fall with a rhythmic insistence, gigantic, silvery tanks
squat in the background, and the metallic croak of Quinlan's voice as it
ricochets out of the recording machine held by Vargas overlays the
scene with a nightmarish confusion. Vargas himself clambers after the
two men, finally wading beneath a bridge to keep within range of the
microphone hidden in Menzies's clothing. When Quinlan senses the
presence of Vargas, and his friend's complicity, he shoots Menzies.
Symbolically, he tries to bathe his hand free of blood in the slimy,
cluttered water in which Vargas has just been standing. One thinks
of the moment in *The Lady from Shanghai* when Grisby smears his
blood over O'Hara's clothes to incriminate him more effectively.

This sequence, like the first one at the border, and the murder of
Grandi, takes place at night. *Touch of Evil* is essentially a film of the
darkness; the blend of shadow and silhouette emphasises the vague,
intangible nature of the intrigue itself, and the darkness offers a cloak
for crime and revenge. As Gilles Jacob has argued, "What does it
matter if the shadow is arbitrary, if the lighting is arbitrary; all that
counts is the dramatic illusion thus attained."[91]

Seen in the context of Welles's other work, *Touch of Evil* is a most
revealing film. Sergei Gerasimov, the Soviet director, has said of it:
"This depressing, and I would say most amoral film had all the characteristics of present-day decadence in art. In the realm of ideas it
flaunts lack of faith in man, a squeamish aversion for him, while in the

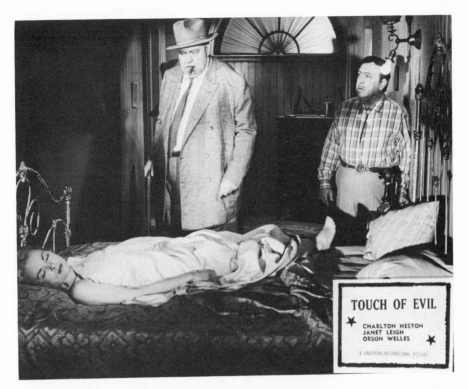

TOUCH OF EVIL

★ CHARLTON HESTON
JANET LEIGH
ORSON WELLES ★

A UNIVERSAL INTERNATIONAL PICTURE

Above, Quinlan and Grandi (Akim Tamiroff) with the drugged wife of Vargas. Below, Quinlan about to kill Grandi.

1851-37

The final sequence of TOUCH OF EVIL. Above, Vargas adjusts his radio set as Menzies and Quinlan's conversation reaches him. Below, Vargas wades beneath the bridge as Quinlan continues to "confess."

sphere of artistic form it shows a morbid confusion, a shift of realistic concepts towards metaphysics, towards the dissecting room and the 'aesthetics' of filth and blood."[86] But surely the point of Welles's view of the world is that goodness can be perceived through evil? For all his grotesqueness, Quinlan is more human a figure than any Gerasimov has created, and *Touch of Evil* runs true to the great tragedies of literature, from Sophocles and Euripides to Shakespeare and Marlowe. The study of corruption is no less valid than the study of innocence.

Welles is aware that one of his major themes is "the struggle for dignity. I absolutely disagree with those works of art, those novels, those films that, these days, speak about despair. I do not think that an artist may take total despair as a subject: we are too close to it in daily life."[29] While this may sound as arbitrary as Gerasimov's remarks, it shows that like all great artists Welles is eager to cut his moorings and let his fancy free—to escape from everyday reality and yet help one to bear with it through contact with a world of the imagination.

THE TRIAL

"Prague does not let you out
of its grip; it has claws, and
whoever wanted to shake himself free of this town would
have to set fire to it!"—
FRANZ KAFKA in a letter[112]

PLOT OUTLINE—Joseph K is awakened and ar-
raigned by police officers early one morning. They
refuse to name his offence. The officers put him under
"open" arrest and leave. He talks about his predicament
with Mrs. Grubach, his landlady, and Miss Burstner,
his neighbour. At his office, he is rebuked by his Deputy
Manager for associating with his teenage cousin, Irmie.
At the opera, a police inspector leads him away to the
Law Courts where he argues violently with the magistrate. Again at his office he discovers the two police
officers who had arrested him earlier being whipped in
a small room. He ignores their pleas for help, and is
then forced to bear with the admonitions of his Uncle
Max. The latter leads him to his acquaintance, Hastler
the Advocate. Hastler is sick and his mistress, Leni, is
attracted to Joseph K. Joseph returns to the empty Law
Courts and has an amorous interlude with Hilda, wife
of one of the guards. He next meets the courtroom
guard who introduces him to a crowd of accused men,
awaiting a hearing. This sends him hurrying back to
Hastler's quarters where one of the Advocate's long-
suffering clients, Block, is a witness to his indifference
and underlying impotence. Joseph decides to dispense
with the Advocate's services and is advised by Leni to
consult Titorelli, the court painter, about his case. This
new character is as depressing as the others, and Joseph
flees a crowd of children outside his studio until, via
subterranean passages, he finds himself in a huge cathedral. A priest tells him he has been condemned and

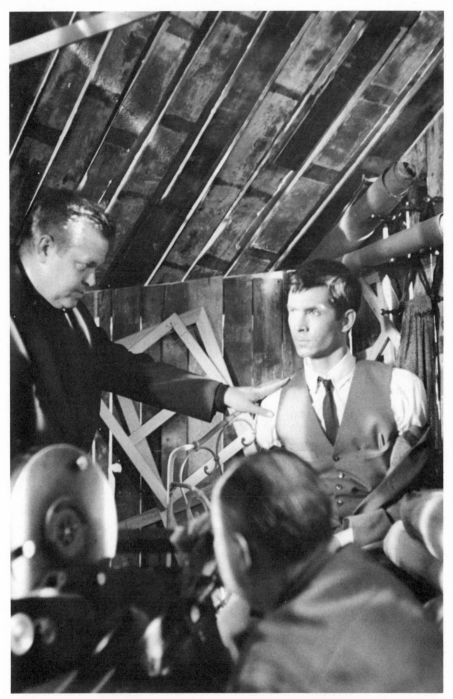

Welles directs Anthony Perkins as Joseph K in THE TRIAL. Photo by Nicolas Tikhomiroff/Uniphoto.

Hastler, suddenly putting in an appearance, recounts
to him the allegory of the man who seeks admittance
to the Law. Joseph is met outside the cathedral by two
executioners. They lead him away across some waste
land and force him to strip in a quarry. They pass a
knife over him from one to the other, and when he
refuses to kill himself they leave the quarry and toss a
bunch of dynamite down to him. K laughs and hurls
something back. There is a great explosion.

THE TRIAL WAS THE FIRST FILM since *Citizen Kane* to be
released in the form that Welles intended. It was hailed as a masterpiece
by a majority of continental critics. With few exceptions, it was dismissed as a boring failure by the British and American press. To my
mind, *The Trial* remains Welles's finest film since *Kane* and, far from
being a travesty of Kafka's work, achieves an effect through cinematic
means that conveys perfectly the terrifying vision of the modern world
that marks every page of the original book (first published, incidentally,
in 1925, two years after Kafka's death).

During the winter of 1959–60 Welles was playing the role of Fulton
in Abel Gance's *Austerlitz*. The producer was the astute Alexander
Salkind and he offered Welles 650 million francs with which to make
a film of *The Trial*. The script took Welles about six weeks to write.
The film was eventually shot in 1962 and, though rumour had it that
it would appear at Venice that year, it did not open in Paris until just
after Christmas. "I don't know why there was any fuss about the film's
not being shown at Venice," says Welles. "There were still some scenes
that had to be shot. Perkins had to do a film with Cayatte [*Le Couteau
dans la plaie*/*Five Miles to Midnight*] and he had arranged to shoot
these scenes for *The Trial* afterwards."* In any case, the soundtrack
was incomplete and unsatisfactory.

Most of the film was photographed in Zagreb (but locations in
Dubrava, Rome, and the Gare d'Orsay were also used). The Gare
d'Orsay, scheduled for demolition these past ten years and more, has
sprawled on the Left Bank of the Seine since the turn of the century.
As William Chappell (Titorelli in the film) has recalled: "Welles is
a poor sleeper, and standing sleepless at five in the morning at the
window of his hotel in Paris he became half-hypnotised by the twin
moons of the two great clocks that decorate the deserted and crumbling
Gare d'Orsay, that triumphantly florid example of the Belle Epoque
that looms so splendidly across the trees of the Tuileries gardens. He
remembered he had once been offered the empty station . . . as a location, and his curiosity was aroused."[72] His choice was a stroke of genius.
The monstrous perspectives, dwarfing the characters, the vistas of im-

prisoned glass, the iron stairways and myriad corridors combine to
form a symbolic background to the film that is an equivalent to the
labyrinthine ways and mournful buildings of Prague. "For the shy
Kafka the periphery of Prague was an unexplored, obscure world of
proletarians, even though it began only a few hundred yards from the
Café Arco, where he was a regular. This district, called Zizkov, probably inspired the eerie setting of the 'interrogation' in [the novel]
The Trial."[112]

The Trial is so rich and complex a Wellesian creation that only
a detailed analysis can begin to do justice to it. Initially it should be
stressed that Welles has adapted the novel fairly freely, while at the
same time he has adhered to Kafka's basic views and situations. After
all, Max Brod acted just as arbitrarily when, after Kafka's death, he
arranged the chapters in the order he thought fit. For the record, Claude
Miller[111] maintains that Welles has changed the order of the chapters
to: 1,4,2,5,6,3,8,7,9,10.

The film opens with a remarkable sequence composed of designs
by Alexandre Alexeïeff and his wife on their patent "pin screen." The
figures are not animated; a wise precaution to prevent their assuming
a dramatic, as opposed to an illustrative, effect. Over these "prints," as
it were, Welles narrates the fable that Kafka puts into the mouth of the
priest in the latter part of the book. It contains the theme of the film
in a nutshell and Welles felt that his audience would understand the
film better if they grasped the idea behind it at the outset. "Before the
Law there stands a Guard. A man comes from the country, begging
admittance to the Law. But the Guard cannot admit him . . . for years
he waits. Everything he has he gives away . . ." Eventually, on the
threshold of death, he asks the Guard one final question: "How is it
then, that in all these years, no one else has ever come here seeking
admittance?" The Guard then tells him: "This door was intended
only for you—and now I am going to close it." Welles pauses, then
comments in a heavy, monitory voice, "This tale is told during the
story called 'The Trial.' It has been said that the logic of this story is
the logic of a dream—of a nightmare," and as the last word fades on the
soundtrack, the screen becomes black and gradually fades in on the
head of Joseph K, seen from above as he is disturbed by the police
entering his room. One has the feeling that K awakes (or is *born*)
guilty. Guilt is a disease.

In an unusually long take, K argues with the officers who come
to arrest him. The use of reflected light through the window gives the
scene a grey, sombre effect. The bedroom "has trick perspectives as
though the scene had been painted by a medieval painter; the floor

Joseph K is observed while dressing by an Assistant Inspector (Billy Kearns).

seems to be raked, the ceiling almost presses on his head and people's trunks are too big for their limbs."[88] Immediately, Welles's dialogue has an ambivalent, disconcerting logic that introduces a sinister note into what otherwise might be merely a routine check-up. Every time K trips over his words the officers toss them back at him, pinning him to an offence. The air is heavy with intimidation, and K's anguished query, "The real question is—who accuses me?" hangs unanswered as the officers and the three clerks who have betrayed him surround K blackly. "It's not for me to talk about your case," says the inspector (everyone in society shirks responsibility and the Advocate is the only one who may state the charge) .

As the scope of the action expands, one notes that Welles has located K's room in an ultra-modern apartment block, and while he watches the arrival of Miss Burstner from a taxi far below, the buildings seem already to encroach on the human beings in their midst (as in Antonioni's *La Notte*). K's landlady, Mrs. Grubach, is introduced briefly. "With your arrest I get the feeling of something abstract," she muses, thereby stressing a point that is to be reiterated visually throughout the film. K behaves perfectly normally as in the novel, fulfilling Kafka's memorable description: "He had always been inclined to take things easily, to believe in the worst only when the worst happened, to take no care for the morrow even when the outlook was threatening."[93] His encounter with Miss Burstner (not his typist, as in the book, but a cabaret entertainer) emphasises his shyness and vulnerability. He confides to her that when his father accused him as a child, and he was innocent, "I'd still feel guilty." Thus the notion of a pre-ordained guilt, or of Original Sin, creeps insidiously into the film (as it does into *Macbeth*). K, in Welles's eyes, stands for a society that is to blame for the ghastly knots into which it has tied itself. "In my opinion, for Kafka, Joseph K was guilty. For me also . . . he is guilty because he is part of the human condition."[27] At the same time he moulds into the pattern Welles usually imposes on his films; he approximates to Leland, to O'Hara, to Van Stratten in his gullibility. As he says bitterly when he glances at the books in the courtroom later, "Of course I must remain ignorant of any law."

Now one comes to one of the most staggering scenes in Welles's cinema. The camera follows Joseph K into the office—in the novel, a bank—where he works; and then tracks—almost hovers—beside him to reveal a vast exposition hall filled with typists seated at hundreds of desks in all directions. The noise of the thousands of keys tapping away is magnified together with long musical chords on the soundtrack so that K seems virtually to drown in the cacophony. The image, such a *frisson* in itself, is a masterly reminder of a bureaucracy gone mad. K lives in a bureaucratic society, where everything has a reference, and everything is referred to someone else. Welles rented between 700–850 typewriters from the Olivetti company and found the gigantic building just outside Zagreb. By contrast to this frenzied, futuristic activity, the storeroom where K leaves a cake he has bought for Miss Burstner's birthday is dusty and oppressive. He is surprised there by his Deputy Manager who, when he sees a girl trying to attract K's attention through the glass walls of the building, thinks she is his mistress. She is in fact K's cousin, Irmie. But this misunderstanding, which contributes to K's sense of shame and isolation, is only one of a number of incidents hinting at eroticism that Welles has scattered throughout *The Trial*. To a certain extent, the women in the film are all temptresses in the tradition of Elsa Bannister. They weaken K's resistance

Miss Burstner (Jeanne Moreau) returns from her night club. Note the use of ceilinged sets, so often a feature of Welles's work.

and draw him inexorably towards his doom with their blandishments or accusations.

The scene now moves to a stretch of waste land near K's office. It is dusk, and K carries on a Pinterish conversation about free will with Miss Pittl (a friend of Miss Burstner's), who is dragging a trunk from one building to another. The camera accompanies the couple as they move slowly over this eerie landscape, K trying desperately to ingratiate himself with this woman and she—like nearly everyone else in the film—rejecting him suspiciously. He ends by admitting responsibility for Miss Burstner's being turned out of her lodgings. Welles's talent lies of course in making K a sympathetic character while at the same

K with Miss Burstner in her room.

Welles rehearses the office sequence, with row upon row of Olivettis in the background. Photo by Nicolas Tikhomiroff/Uniphoto.

time giving credence to his detractors' viewpoint. This dismal scene, with the mournful howling of dogs in the background, foreshadows the end when Joseph K is led away to his death, also in the gathering dusk. It is in this sequence (consisting of one long take) also that one can distinguish the difference between the style of Kafka and the style of Welles. In the words of Elliott Stein, "Kafka's novels presents a rather realistically described world—but it is inhabited by dream people. . . . In Welles's film real people inhabit a nightmare world."[129] Every image holds a portent, every conversation a veiled threat. Thus in the next sequence, after K has been called from the opera, there is a clear clue to his fate. The inspector leads him from the opera house (and, by

Joseph K in conversation with Miss Pittl. A Zagreb apartment block in the background.

K is summoned from the opera by the Inspector (Arnoldo Foà).

implication, from the normal surroundings that might prevent him from losing his reason), and pauses in a derelict hall. Welles's script describes these buildings as "monumental in aspect but dilapidated, sinister and cold. They exude the melancholy atmosphere of all public institutions."[6] Two men stand in the shadows. They are wearing raincoats and squat, baleful hats. One has glasses like pebbles. The inspector tells K the way to the court, now in session, and, when K asks sarcastically why the two silent men should not follow him, watching his every move, he is blandly assured, "That isn't their job." Their "job," as one finds out later, is to kill Joseph K.

Like a man lost in a maze, K pursues the twists and turns of the

Joseph K walks among the numbered prisoners of the Law, dwarfed by a shrouded statue.

route. Suddenly he comes upon a girl, Hilda, who is washing clothes. She nods in the direction of the door to the tribunal. K opens it and the camera swoops in behind him. This moment is one of the most terrifying in the film, for precisely as K enters one hears the roar of hundreds of feet as everyone in the packed courtroom stands up and stares at him. And now the long takes used hitherto give way to staccato cutting; Welles shows the court and its occupants from many different angles, rather like the election speech scene in *Citizen Kane*. It is interesting to recall Kafka's description of the event: "K felt as though he were entering a meeting-hall. A crowd of the most variegated people—nobody troubled about the newcomer—filled a medium sized, two-windowed room, which just below the roof was surrounded by a

K screams at the court.

gallery, also quite packed, where the people were able to stand only in a bent posture with their heads and backs knocking against the ceiling."[93] The film differs only in that everyone *does* trouble about the arrival of Joseph K and this, visually speaking, underlines the hostility shown towards him. He is guilty in advance and human society, represented in the court, regards him as a scapegoat. He belongs, like all else, to the court. His apologia on the platform beside the magistrate is worthless. He is doomed in advance and the violent manner in which Hilda is suddenly carried out by the Law student seems to carry a foretaste of K's own destruction. The monstrous door of the courtroom dwarfs him as he leaves.

The fast cutting between shots continues until the end of the film.

Again, the individual's proportions are reduced, as K leaves the courtroom.

K tries desperately to escape from the "whipping room."

The storm, as it were, has broken about K's head. In the early part he had still not been engulfed. But from now on his sole preoccupation is with his case. Back at his office he finds that the two officers who had arrested him the previous morning are about to be flogged in a lumber-room because K had complained of their stealing his shirts. In this nightmarish scene, with everyone talking at once and the whipper snarling like a predatory animal eager to consume his victims, still more guilt seems to transfer itself to K and to weigh on his conscience. One should never forget that one clear implication of both the book and the film is that K is made aware of his guilt by suggestion. Welles, having lived through an epoch where the torture chamber and the concentration camp became law, has, not unnaturally, a more bitter viewpoint than Kafka's. Joseph K is all the more responsible because he

The Advocate, Hastler (Orson Welles) with Leni (Romy Schneider).

does not and cannot stop the whipping. The music of Albinoni, detached from the action and opposed to the flurried montage (some shots last only a few frames) lends an air of inevitability to the sequence.

Welles himself plays the crucial role of Hastler, the Advocate, to whom his Uncle Max leads K after hearing about the case. Once again, the *décor* has an importance of its own. Hastler's long, lofty chambers are illuminated by hundreds of candles, as if signifying the eternal vigilance of the Law. The Advocate himself is ill, sprawled on a gilt bed. Leni, his secretary and mistress, places a hot flannel over his face as Uncle Max and Joseph K approach him. When he hears *who* is accused, however, Hastler starts up and peels off the flannel. For a second the steam drifts about his chin and imparts a diabolical look to his face. He represents Lucifer; he is evil incarnate, like Harry Lime or Arthur Bannister. K escapes his gaze and follows the nubile Leni behind a glass partition, to another room. Then she wraps K in one of the Advocate's black coats, metaphorically stifling him in the folds of authority. She shows him how her hand is deformed with a web of skin between the fingers. One remembers Miss Pittl's club foot, and later Irmie is seen dragging her leg down the steps of the court building. The physical warp is an outward and visible sign of the psychological deformity. The prominence given to hands by Welles in this film is fascinating, and recurs in the later scene when Block kisses the Advocate's hand. It is as if the hand were a symbol of tyranny, from whose clutches no one may escape.

Leni talks with K in a huge room filled with aging files and newspapers, and points out a picture of one of the judges. "He's little, almost a dwarf," she whispers, "but look at the way he had himself painted." This is the nearest K ever comes to encountering those responsible for his fate; he is always fobbed off with the *accessories* to the Law. A call from Hastler interrupts the love-play, and K stumbles down the mountain of newspapers with his coat fluttering around

Hastler with Joseph K and his Uncle Max (Max Haufler).

him like a Mephistophelian cloak, as though some of the rancid evil of the place had attached itself to him. Then, with a storm raging outside, the immense silhouette of the Advocate moves behind the glass partition of the junk room, demonstrating his impalpability and shadowy power.

Suddenly, quite by chance, Joseph K catches his first glimpe of Block. He peers into a cell-like room and sees the old man seated on a bed. The flash of apprehension vanishes as Leni interrupts, but in that moment when Block's eyes meet his, K has foreseen his fate. Block might as well be a prefigurement of K in twenty years' time, downtrodden by the Law, bereft of all will to escape, resigned to perpetual imprisonment—the man come from the country to seek admittance to the Law, no less.

The erotic element introduced by Welles appears again in the next scene, when K returns to the empty Law Courts. Hilda meets him there and as they talk together ("even though it's forbidden") about the tribunal, K glances at one of the judge's textbooks. Immediately he finds a "dirty" picture, a reflection of his own jaundiced imagination (one could argue at length that the entire film is seen through K's eyes and that perfectly normal people and events are distorted by his mind). The accent is again on eroticism as Hilda strokes K's ankles and tries to seduce him. Their conversation is interrupted when a student guard comes and carries Hilda off on his shoulders. As he clambers towards them through the supports of the platform in the courtroom, there is an echo of Kafka's *Metamorphoses*: spars and struts seem to merge with the snarling man and give him the look of a beast of prey. Then, as if pursued by this vivid image (and bars are as important in *The Trial* as they are in *Othello*), K shortly afterwards sees another man approaching him along a catwalk below the roof of the Gare d'Orsay like a spider leaving his web. He vents his anger on K. Talking of the student who has abducted his wife, Hilda, he says slowly and with infinite sadism: "I would have squashed him flat against the wall long ago . . . all twisted out and writhing—like a smashed cockroach." The last word is savoured carefully and floats menacingly in the air. Here one can again prove that Welles is faithful to the spirit of Kafka's dialogue. In the book the Guard says, "I see him squashed flat there, just a little above the floor, his arms wide, his fingers spread, his bandy legs writhing in a circle, and splashes of blood all around."[93] At the same time one discerns the persistent undercurrent of *jealousy* that runs through the book and still more strongly through the film. It is as if everyone is possessive in the extreme, Hastler of Leni, the Guard of his wife, K of Leni with Block, and Irmie of K.

Hilda (Elsa Martinelli) is led away from K by her student boy friend (Thomas Holtzmann).

Joseph K now has his first encounter with the other fugitives from the Law like himself. "The accused," says the Guard, as he points out to K an entire hall filled with silent men. K talks with one of them and is frustrated by his naïve, trusting attitude. "You think I'm a— judge?" asks K fearfully. One sees in this particular old man an exact personification of the supplicant in the prologue. "Yes, I handed in several affidavits," he tells K. "That was some time ago. I'm waiting here for the result." The words could also belong to Block.

When even those in the same predicament as himself begin to doubt him, K realises that his case is hopeless. Like the destitute figures who surround the shrouded statue of Christ on K's way to the tribunal

K among "the Accused." This still shows Welles's masterly use of the Gare d'Orsay as a location.

earlier in the film, these mute captives hint at a lost harmony in the world, over and above their immediate significance *vis-à-vis* the Nazi concentration camps. K flees this hideous waiting room and it is now that one can appreciate Welles's brilliant dovetailing of locations. K walks out of the Gare d'Orsay to discover that outside, on the steps of the Palazzo di Giustizia in Rome, his cousin Irmie is waiting for him. They walk together to the entrance of a Milan factory, he says goodbye to her, and a few seconds later approaches the council house in Zagreb where he lives.[129] Irmie's presence is valid, for she is the only "normal" person (excepting Mrs. Grubach) in the entire film—thus the simple replies she gives to K when she wants to marry him. "But I'm your cousin," he says, aghast. Irmie: "Cousins get married." K:

Buildings seem to press in on Joseph K.

"You wouldn't want to marry a criminal?" Irmie: "Crooks get married too." Her interventions are like those of Shakespeare's clowns. They anchor the drama in normality and also serve to heighten the bizarre feeling of ensuing scenes.

The next sequence, involving Katina Paxinou as a scientist, was cut from the final version of the film; not surprisingly, because the final lines of the script here hint that the crime K is most likely to commit is suicide. Instead the scene switches to the Advocate's rooms once more. The theme of the film is growing noticeably more serious, and there is a brief interlude while K and Block writhe in uncontrollable laughter about the old man's having five other Advocates of whom he never tells Hastler. Then, as K is about to be interviewed by the Advocate, Block says, chillingly, that he is only being received because his case is still at "the hopeful stage." Block, then, is a symbol of a man crushed by the Law and its intolerable burden. K dies because he openly rejects the Advocate. Block survives because he acquiesces in the situation—he hires his five other Advocates secretly, but he survives—nourished, presumably, by his furtive liaison with Leni. As Kafka wrote: "So the Advocate's methods, to which K fortunately had not been long enough exposed, amounted to this: that the client finally forgot the whole world and lived only in hope of toiling along this false path until the end of his case should come in sight."[93] Block, like everyone else, shies away from mentioning the nature of the charges— "They even say that he's [Hastler] a better Advocate for business . . . than for *the other kind*" (my italics), rather as "cancer" is a word to be avoided at all costs in contemporary conversation.

When K enters the Advocate's presence (significantly, he and Block do not wear their coats on entry), the pace of the film begins to accelerate—and never slows again. This time Hastler's attitude has hardened;

K hurries up the stairs to Titorelli's studio, accompanied by squealing children.

there is a threat behind the velvet voice: "You can pick out an accused man in the largest crowd," and that final remark of Welles's own invention: "To be in chains is sometimes safer than to be free." K, repulsed by the sight of Block, kissing Hastler's hands and crying "Master!" to him, rushes out, with the braying, demoniac laughter of the Advocate pursuing him. It is a decisive moment. Block has described the Advocate as "a very revengeful man," and K's rejection of his services marks him as a man to be eliminated. He, K, can no longer be identified with the man in the prologue. Leni advises him to see Titorelli, the court painter, and in desperation K seeks him out. He is followed up ladders and a narrow spiral staircase by a flock of screaming children. Some critics have said that Welles's touch is too heavy here, but a glance at Kafka's text shows that although the scene has been altered visually, its overall impact has not been exaggerated. "In the tenement where the painter lived only one wing of the great double door stood open, and beneath the other wing, in the masonry near the ground, there was a gaping hole out of which, just as K approached, issued a disgusting yellow fluid, steaming hot, from which a rat fled into the adjoining canal. At the foot of the stairs an infant lay bellydown on the ground bawling, but one could scarcely hear its shrieks because of the deafening din that came from a tinsmith's workshop at the other side of the entry."[93]

When K eventually reaches Titorelli's studio, he finds himself in a kind of wooden cage, the bars of which encroach on him. The children peep through the cracks, and Titorelli shoos them away, tossing off a disturbing "Remember my ice pick?" to one of them, and then rounds unexpectedly on K with a glib "What can I do for you, chum?" (the camera dollies back suddenly to emphasise K's shock). The terrifying atmosphere of the studio weighs on K. The children rustling outside like impatient birds, the sinister hum in the background, and the almost stifling heat, prevent him from assimilating Titorelli's elaborate disquisition on "ostensible acquittal." He puts on a pair of spectacles to look closely at the artist's work, and again one is reminded of *Metamorphoses*—K's face is for an instant seemingly transmogrified into that of a beetle.

Titorelli shows him some paintings; one, of Justice and Victory reunited, prompts K to think of "the goddess of the Hunt . . . in full cry." Everyone in the film is divided, in fact, into hunters and the hunted. One feels that Titorelli, too, is a hunter beneath his gleaming charm. K bursts out of the studio and finds himself in the Law Courts office. It is a point of betrayal, like the Knight's discovery that he has been "confessing" to Death in the church in *The Seventh Seal*. K

Joseph K with Titorelli (William Chappell). Note the stripes of light used so effectively by Welles. Photo by Nicolas Tikhomiroff/Uniphoto.

brushes past a group of men awaiting trial in the archive room and then rushes down a subterranean passage. As he runs, the children pursue him, their screams filling the soundtrack. Stripes of light flood through the slatted corridor and make a dancing, abstract pattern on K's body as he dashes towards the camera (which was being pushed by a Yugoslav runner!). "We built it out of wood, and put the camera on a wheelchair—it was the only way we could move it along the wooden planks."* The effect is astonishing. K is literally absorbed into his surroundings; he is completely disorientated, like O'Hara as he is swept down the "Crazy House" at the end of *The Lady from Shanghai.* Reverse tracking shots sweep back alternatively in front of K and in front of the children as they plunge through one passage after another, their shadows writhing on the walls in a manner reminiscent of that final chase in the sewers of Vienna (*The Third Man*). The sequence runs less than half a minute, but contains some twenty-five closely-knit shots.

K no longer knows where he is going; he is caught in the net of the Law. His flight leads him into a huge cathedral (though even here Welles strikes a frightening note by covering the pillars of the building with tactile rivets), where a priest in a pulpit warns him how badly his case is going. The Advocate also makes an unexpected appearance, and projects on a screen the allegory of the Law with which the film began. There is a memorable moment here as K, caught in the light from the projector, is superimposed before the gates of the Law like the man in the story. And when Hastler repeats the words of the Guard, "And now I'm going to close it [the door]," the audience, though not K, senses that Hastler himself *is* the Guard. Once more, and for the last time, K breaks away. As he passes the priest on his way out of the cathedral, the latter asks him, "Can't you see anything at all?" "Of course," replies K, "I'm responsible." "My son—" begins the priest. "I'm not your son," snarls K fiercely. In these two answers lies the key to *The Trial*: on the one hand, the cry of an entire world in the knowledge that it is guilty of allowing such an evil administration to gain power (Hastler: "A victim of society?" K in response: "I'm a *member* of society") ; and on the other the defiant gesture of a Wellesian hero, refusing to surrender meekly in the style of Block.

So to the *dénouement*. K emerges into the dusk and is confronted by the two police officers he had so innocently thought to be his escorts on his first visit to the tribunal. They take his arms and then lead him away brusquely. So carefully has Welles followed the novel at this juncture that Kafka's own words are the best description of the scene: "K walked rigidly between them, the three of them were interlocked in a unity which would have brought all three down together had one of them been knocked over. It was a unity such as can be formed by lifeless elements alone."[93] The noble chords of Albinoni's Adagio swell above the scene as the trio pass through the streets and across some waste land to a quarry. "K's route to the execution can be traced from the old town, across Karls Bridge, 'through steeply rising streets'—Neruda Street and Uvoz—to the old Strahover Quarry (which no longer exists) ."[112] There is a strange visual dignity in this last journey that is, perhaps appropriately, lacking in other sequences of the film.

Welles's end is radically different to Kafka's. The final sentence of the book: " 'Like a dog!' he said: it was as if he meant the shame of it to outlive him,"[93] implies a defeatism that Welles cannot accept, and that would be contradicted had Welles retained the scientist's earlier forecast that the crime K is most likely to commit is . . . suicide. In the film K shouts defiantly, "You'll have to do it!" when the killers scramble out of the quarry. He refuses to take the knife from them because he is too aware of the injustice of the sentence. Rightly, the last shot of K is of his laughing with an almost insane glee as he reaches for the dynamite that has been flung down beside him. There is a mighty explosion, and over the grim waste land rises a cloud of smoke

The angled close-up is characteristic of Welles's style.

that assumes the shape of a mushroom. It dissolves into nothingness as Welles reads the cast list. This final image has been another butt for the critics' attacks. Yet the cloud is no more irrelevant or fatalistic than the closing shot of the street lamp in Antonioni's *The Eclipse.* Both images can assume whatever meaning the spectator ascribes to them. The main impression is one of complete finality, catastrophe, waste, physical death.

Apart from *Citizen Kane* and *Chimes at Midnight,* no other film of Welles's bears so clearly the stamp of his personality. One perceives his presence in every frame, in every shadow, in every angled shot. He dubbed no fewer than eleven of the speaking parts, the main one (apart from Hastler) being Titorelli, and others including the magistrate, K's Deputy Manager, and the man with the whip. The key to the style of the film lies in the subjective track and dolly, repeated in endless permutations. Welles is not a *reflective* director here, and the richness of his imagery in *The Trial* precludes any attempt to ponder on the deeper implications of the *décor* or various incidents. It is the immediate and then the cumulative effect that counts. *The Trial* is an expressionist film if expressionism can be described according to Carl Hauptmann's dictum: "The phenomena on the screen are the phenomena of the soul." But whereas most expressionist films ignore the importance of the soundtrack, *The Trial* gains largely from the imaginative blend of music and natural noises that Welles has arranged. Jazz seems suddenly suitable when juxtaposed with classical music, just as the modern buildings of Zagreb merge successfully with the baroque of the Gare d'Orsay. Anthony Perkins as Joseph K gives one of the best performances of his career. Resembling Kafka himself, he suggests with every movement and facial contortion the perplexity that undermines Joseph K in the book. "The human mind isn't that complex," complained Albert Schweitzer to the author when he returned to him a copy of *The Trial*. But human society *is* as complex as Kafka maintained, and the inability of the human mind to understand that complexity is the tragic moral of the novel and of this extraordinary, hallucinatory film.

CHIMES AT MIDNIGHT/FALSTAFF

"I think Falstaff is like a
Christmas tree decorated with
vices. The tree itself is total
innocence and love"
—ORSON WELLES[36]

PLOT OUTLINE—Sir John Falstaff lives at the Boar's
Head Tavern in Eastcheap, which is managed by Mistress Quickly. He is continually drunk and laden with
debts, but he revels in the company of young Prince
Hal, the heir to the English throne. Hal is regarded with
despair and scorn by his father, the opportunist Henry
IV, whose hold over the crown is precarious and hotly
disputed. Falstaff and Hal, together with the Prince's
companion, Poins, indulge in mischievous capers together, and rob some pilgrims at Gadshill. But when
Worcester and the Percy family take up arms against
Henry, life becomes different. There is a crucial battle
at Shrewsbury, from which the King and his men
emerge triumphant. Hal has killed his arch-rival, Hotspur, in a duel, and grows more and more intolerant
of Falstaff and his flaws. When the king dies, Falstaff
believes that his bosom friend, the Prince, will elevate
him and his sort to high office. But instead Hal rejects
the past and has Falstaff banished. As Henry V prepares
to lead his army against the French, news comes of
Falstaff's death.

CHIMES AT MIDNIGHT had been a project of Welles's for twenty-
five years, and his stage presentation of the Falstaff story in Belfast
in 1960 was a prelude to the film version. Shooting began in Spain
in the autumn of 1964 and continued in the second half of 1965 after
Emiliano Piedra and Angel Escolano, film producer and lawyer re-
spectively, covered the budget. Harry Saltzman also invested in *Chimes
at Midnight,* in return for distribution rights, and after fourteen weeks

Welles as Falstaff and Jeanne Moreau as Doll Tearsheet in CHIMES AT MIDNIGHT. Photo by Nicolas Tikhomiroff/Uniphoto.

of shooting, in a wide variety of locations (the Boar's Head Tavern was built in a Madrid basement, Henry's castle was found in the northern Catalans), the film was screened at the Cannes Festival in 1966, where Welles was awarded a special XXth Anniversary prize by the jury.

"What is difficult about Falstaff," believes Welles, "is that he is the greatest conception of a good man, the most completely good man, in all drama. His faults are so small and he makes tremendous jokes out of little faults. But his goodness is like bread, like wine . . ."[28] Critics who complain that Falstaff and the film are not sufficiently rumbustious have a superficial notion of one of Shakespeare's most tragic figures. A men of the world, Falstaff is not easily disillusioned and when, at Hal's coronation, he is rejected in earnest, the shock is too much for even his stout heart. The end of Falstaff implies for Welles the end of an era, the end of chivalry, of "Merrie England." Hal's cynical pragmatism represents the professional approach to life that carries him (as Henry V) to victory over the French. Yet for

Falstaff (and, one feels, for Welles), friendship and personal loyalty are more important than public glory.

To discover the reasons for Falstaff's downfall, one must interpret the relationships set out by history, by Shakespeare, and finally by Welles. Richard II was murdered in 1399. Bolingbroke had declared himself King Henry IV while Mortimer, the true heir to the throne, was in a Welsh prison. But Welles's Henry has none of the arrogance and little of the ruthlessness attributed him by history. He is lean and bitter, holding more admiration for Henry "Hotspur" Percy, Mortimer's brother-in-law, than for his son, Prince Hal (though in reality Hotspur was a year or two older than the King himself). He looks on Hal as "wanton and effeminate," and equates him with his former foe, Richard II. "As thou art to this hour was Richard then /When I from France set foot at Ravenspurgh; And even as I was is Percy now. /Now, by my sceptre and my soul to boot, /He hath more worthy interest to the state /Than thou the shadow of succession."

And Hotspur *does* behave in the film like a young Falstaff—loud, rash, and impetuous, if blessed with a reflective melancholy and a lyric tongue. Welles surrounds him with gusto. As he argues with his uncle and Northumberland at Windsor, he strides in and out of frame, cloak sweeping across each composition like a gesture of energy and frustration. At such moments Welles displays his peerless habit of expanding the screen, by setting people at extremities from one another, foreshortening figures from a low angle, and giving plastic emphasis to verticals such as pillars, trees, and pikes. When Hotspur is next seen, brandishing a letter in his bath-tub, the soundtrack is punctuated with his exclamations and impatient curses. As he dries himself and prepares to leave Warkworth, upflung trumpets blare from the battlements, echoing Hotspur's flatulent bravado, affording an ironic counterpoint for his reluctant virility towards Kate, and heralding his desire for "bloody noses and cracked crowns."

Welles captures the bawdy side of Shakespeare in this sequence, as he does in the Boar's Head, with Pistol threatening every woman in sight with his phallic dagger-sheath and then disappearing into what can only be described as a somewhat public privy. The pigs roaming in the streets and the straw spread on the tavern floor help to convey the essential coarseness of Fifteenth century life, the source of much Falstaffian wit.

The future character of English life, grave or gay, depends on the outcome of the fight between Hal and Hotspur at Shrewsbury. Hal appears to his father and to the world as the relative of Falstaff, but in reality he is only an acquaintance. Though they never meet on

Hotspur (Norman Rodway) with his wife (Marina Vlady).

screen, Falstaff and Hotspur are the true relatives. When Falstaff
arrives at the royal position after the battle, he bears Percy's body
on his back. Hal stares in astonishment, not just with fury at Falstaff's
daring to claim Percy's death, but with an understanding that his
dead foe's spirit endures in Falstaff, whom he had left for dead on
the battlefield. At this precise moment, the Prince determines to sever
all links with the companion of his youth. Welles holds the camera
for long seconds on Henry's face as he observes the dead Percy, and
his son disputing with Falstaff. The King's expression is hardly one of
relief or gratitude. On the contrary, he appears crestfallen at Hotspur's
death, and from now on he moves listlessly towards death.

★ ★ ★

The film expresses the two kinds of basic human tragedy. On the
one hand there is the much-panged solitude of the "responsible" man,
the ruler, the chief executive. This state has often been described in
films, from *Queen Christina* and *Ivan the Terrible* to *Seven Days in
May* and *Fail Safe*. Welles conveys solitude in *Chimes at Midnight*

with the same blend of visual and sound effects as he did in *Citizen Kane*. Henry's Windsor, like Kane's Xanadu, has no relationship with the outside world. The walls are high and massive, the sunbeams from the windows are moted with dust like the arid interior of the Thatcher Memorial Library. There are scarcely any furnishings. In short, the castle resembles nothing so much as a prison, and a cold and draughty one at that. Welles directs Gielgud with such discretion in the "sleep" soliloquy that Henry's despair seems to proceed quite naturally from his situation and surroundings. The King squints at the light beyond the bars of his window. As he talks, the black shadow of the central bar falls on his eyes, oppressing him, caging him as the Knight is caged when he confesses to Death in *The Seventh Seal,* to such a palpable degree that when Welles cuts unexpectedly to a long shot of Gielgud in the same position, the final lines: "Then happy low, lie down! Uneasy lies the head that wears a crown," strike one almost as a relief, even as they counterpoint the isolation of the monarch.

In contrast to this, there is the full-blooded, if just as tragic, figure of Falstaff. In his off moments—the strolls in the snow with Shallow,

"The castle resembles nothing so much as a prison." Henry IV (John Gielgud) is lit from a single window.

Capers in disguise at Gadshill (Falstaff unmistakably at right).

the reflective hours before the fire in Eastcheap with Silence and Shallow conducting a wholly useless conversation across his enormous paunch—Falstaff appears as desolate as the King. But while Henry's castle is overcast with the gloom of duty, Falstaff makes the Boar's Head Tavern resound with gaiety and celebration. The camera too is inert when Henry speaks and proclaims his despair; in Eastcheap it roves, glides, and swings in time with Falstaff's mirth. Falstaff's boisterous approach to life gathers everyone up in its grasp and sends them tumbling downstairs or bounding over Gadshill's autumn leaves. Welles communicates this Saturnalian atmosphere not merely with visual panache, but also by accelerating the pace of the dialogue. Henry's speeches are long, measured, and carefully enunciated. Falstaff's conversations with Doll Tearsheet, Mistress Quickly, Poins or Pistol, are lightning fast, as if each were trying to score off the other. Falstaff, despite his ingenuous air, is always ready with a pun or riposte (*cf* the entire recruiting scene). When the Lord Chief Justice gives a parting shot such as, "God send the Prince a better companion!" his butt retorts, "God send the companion a better Prince!"

Welles's Falstaff does not savour his repartee. He gallops on to

Falstaff is teased by his Prince (Keith Baxter).

the next joke without pausing, subsisting on his wit like the professional jester he is, bored by silence and solemnity as much as by Silence and Shallow.

Though to Elizabethan audiences Falstaff might have been the personification of Vice—gluttony, idleness and lechery all easily discernible in his character—he was a well-loved amalgam of temptations too. Welles, tailor-made for the role (give or take a few cushions for girth's sake) embodies Falstaff's beneficent qualities. As A. R. Humphreys has written, "He is vicious, yet his vices are a tonic for human nature; he exploits his dependants, yet they remain indissolubly attached to him; he lies, yet would be dismayed if his lies were to be believed. He laments his age, corpulence, and lost agility, yet he behaves with the gaiety of youth, has intellectual legerity to offset his bulk, and is agile whenever it suits him."*

Welles conveys Falstaff's hedonistic spirit by retaining the long paean to sack; by underlining his participation in any escapade (such

---

* A. R. Humphreys: "The First Part of *King Henry IV*" (The Arden Shakespeare, Methuen, London 1960)

as Gadshill, where Falstaff is as clearly exploited as the unfortunate pilgrims) ; and by returning to him again and again during the Battle of Shrewsbury, soup ladle suspended above a cauldron, steamy breath filtering through his helmet as he feigns death beside the fallen Hotspur. For all his rejection at the climax of the film, Falstaff has taught his beloved Hal as much about life as anyone. The King has usurped the crown and suffers bitterly from it; Falstaff tries to take credit for many lesser feats (dispatching seven "men in buckram" in the woods, fighting "a long hour by Shrewsbury clock" with Harry Percy) , but his conscience is clear as day. While others, less endowed with imagination and aplomb, fight to the death, Falstaff's most violent act is to chase Pistol downstairs at the Boar's Head (Welles deliberately does not show his stabbing of Hotspur's corpse) . On the brink of battle, he confides in his friend, "I would it were bed-time, Hal, and all well." He is a rogue, and still there is often more wisdom in his advice than in the magniloquent speeches of Henry or the Prince—when, for instance, he urges Hal to beware of Poins, or claims that, "Honour is a mere scutcheon." Weighed down by debt, deserted by Hal and the rest, Falstaff dies, babbling of green fields, with his nose as sharp as any pen. "The fuel is gone that maintained that fire," mutters Bardolph as he and Nym push the heavy coffin away under a cloud-banked sky, and Ralph Richardson intones Holinshed's description of the new King—"a pattern in princehood, a lodestar to honour, and famous to the world alway." A bitter comment in context, for Hal's youth and natural exuberance are as dead as Falstaff. "Thou'lt forget me when I'm gone," are his words to Doll Tearsheet in the tavern; like all hedonists, Falstaff has illusions about everything save death. And Bardolph's remark is plainly significant in Welles's opinion, for Falstaff *is* a fire set against the cold that pervades the film—the cold of Henry's castle, the chill wind of the battlefield, the snows that prompt Shallow to recall "the chimes at midnight," and the autumn woods of Gadshill.

★   ★   ★

The film can be approached from another direction. For those familiar with Welles's career, *Chimes at Midnight* may appear as a further illustration of the "scorpion-frog" story told in *Confidential Report*. According to this scheme, Hal is the "scorpion" whose nature compels him to sting Falstaff, the "frog" who bears him so cheerfully over the river of youth. Although Shakespeare (who undoubtedly felt that Hal's behaviour was not so much noxious as shrewd, part of the

"Thou'lt forget me when I'm gone." Falstaff with Doll in the East-cheap tavern.

process of becoming a disciplined King) did not describe the relation-ship between the two characters in these terms, the original dialogue of the play requires scant distortion for it to fit the Wellesian pattern of things. The Prince is seen in the guise of a predator, Nemesis incarnate; he is to Falstaff as Iago is to Othello, Menzies to Quinlan, Hastler to Joseph K, Georgie Minafer to Isabel. So, while Shakespeare gave his audience—and Falstaff—various pointers to Hal's eventual change of heart towards his old companions, Welles chooses to dwell emphatically on such moments. When Falstaff suggests "a play ex-tempore" in the Boar's Head, the mood is merry and vivacious. But soon Hal seizes the saucepan Falstaff has taken for a crown and proceeds to berate his mentor—"That villanous abominable misleader of youth, Falstaff, that old white-bearded Satan." Falstaff listens in embarrass-ment, defends himself bombastically and then chuckles good-naturedly, "Banish plump Jack, and banish all the world." Hal, face averted, replies in earnest: "I do, I will," speaking as much for his future self as for his father, and Welles lets a significant pause elapse before Bardolph dashes in with news of the Sheriff's arrival. As in *Hamlet,* therefore, the play within a play reveals more truth about the characters than do their orthodox exchanges.

The next intimation of Falstaff's fate comes after the Battle of Shrewsbury. Falstaff calls for sack and proceeds to extol its virtues before the Prince and a crowd of retainers. But Hal's face remains cold and clenched; having disposed of Hotspur, he is poised to abandon both Falstaff and his beloved sack, alike symbols of his dissipated youth. As Falstaff ends his speech—"If I had a thousand sons, the first human principle I would teach them should be to forswear thin potations and to addict themselves to sack,"—the Prince wanders away across the slope to join his cavalry, letting his sack mug drop as he goes. Welles does not have him dash it to the ground with theatrical emphasis; the casual, almost automatic gesture carries far more force, as if Hal were sloughing off his past as the butterfly does its chrysalis. Falstaff, his eyes perplexed by sack, stares after his departing companion.

Falstaff tries a shield for a hat.

Much later, when Hal is summoned from the Boar's Head to attend his dying father at Windsor, Falstaff's face wears the same expression of bewilderment. The Prince strides out of the Tavern through the roistering crowd, but Falstaff is restrained by the females and when he reaches the stables he finds Hal already astride his horse. A last cheery wave from the Prince, and Falstaff stands alone in the gate. "Now comes in the sweetest morsel of the night, and we must leave it unpicked," he muses, presentiment, rather than reason, telling him that the years of fickleness are ended.

So to the final rejection. Falstaff is once again too sure of himself. Learning of Hal's accession, he is elated, scattering premature largesse in all directions. "Master Robert Shallow, choose what office thou wilt in the land, 'tis thine. Pistol, I will charge thee with dignities . . . Happy are they which have been my friends, and woe unto my lord chief justice!" Pushing his way through the men-at-arms at Westminster Abbey, he staggers hopefully into the coronation procession. "God save thee, my sweet boy! My King! My Jove! I speak to thee, my heart!" But for Falstaff, childless and eager to share his Royal "son's" glory, denial is short and sharp. "I know thee not, old man: fall to thy prayers; How ill white hairs become a fool and jester!" replies Hal scornfully. So Falstaff's weakness for living off others has defeated him at last. He is stunned. His jaw trembles, and he musters a faint smile to mask his grief. Had he been more shrewd and circumspect in his approach, he might have earned favours and a living from the new King. Falstaff, like all the great figures in Welles's cinema, must remain true to his nature. A small figure now in the Abbey gates, he rolls disconsolately away to supper, pausing to answer Shallow's whining request for the repayment of a loan—"I will be as good as my word."

Yet Hal, despite his callous cynicism, has some justification for his conduct. By the end of the film, one cannot help feeling that Hal spurns Falstaff in the same way as he has been spurned by his father, Henry IV. Early on, Henry is heard praising Harry Percy at his son's expense. "O! that it could be prov'd /That some night-tripping fairy had exchang'd /In cradle-clothes our children where they lay, /And call'd mine Percy, his Plantagenet. /Then would I have his Henry, and he mine." There's no doubt that the Prince has sown his wild oats early. He suggests to Falstaff that they should "take a purse tomorrow," and lets his evil genius, Poins, work out the details of the Gadshill escapade. But already his father's scorn is secretly gnawing at his pleasure. As he leaves the Boar's Head he pauses to stare beyond the camera: "I know you all, and will awhile uphold /The unyok'd humour

Falstaff at the Abbey.

of your idleness." There is calculation in Hal, where there is none in
Falstaff. Welles places considerable stress on the scene beside the lake
(*Henry IV, Pt 2*, Act 2, Sc 2) when Hal confesses to Poins that he is
concerned about his public image. "But I tell thee my heart bleeds
inwardly that my father is so sick; and keeping such vile company as
thou art hath in reason taken from me all ostentation of sorrow." And
Poins appears in *Chimes at Midnight* with the status almost of a lover,
whose ambivalent lines ("I can stand the push of your one thing," etc.)
bring a sinister note to the film. Hal's final blunder in public is to
take the crown before his father actually dies. "O foolish youth!" cries
Henry, "Thou seek'st the greatness that will overwhelm thee." It is
probably in these painful moments that Hal decides to dispense with
his foibles.

From close-ups of Hal's face beside his dying father's, Welles cuts
to long shots of his announcing Henry's death to the court. He looks
frail and lonely in the moted sunbeams, heir to all those troubled
thoughts that his father has described in the "Uneasy lies the head
that wears a crown" soliloquy a short time before. Even Falstaff, after
his humiliating dismissal in the Abbey, still misreads the Prince. "Do

Poins (Tony Beckley) and Falstaff at Gadshill.

not you grieve at this," he assures Shallow. "I shall be sent for in private to him. Look you, he must seem thus to the world." And forgiveness does follow quickly. "Enlarge the man committed yesterday /That rail'd against our person," Hal tells Exeter as he prepares to lead his troops to France. "We consider /It was excess of wine that set him on." But, like Georgie Minafer's remorse, it is too late a gesture. Falstaff is already in his coffin.

★   ★   ★

Financial exigencies have usually denied Welles the easy means of achieving his effects in colour. But he has never resisted the challenge of filming in monochrome and, from its very first sequence, *Chimes at Midnight* offers thoughtful combinations of black and white. Before the credits, Falstaff and Shallow stumble across a snowy landscape, their scarecrow figures surrounded by the hard whiteness of winter. There is immediately a sense of loneliness, loss, and nostalgia, evoking the ride in the snow in *The Magnificent Ambersons,* or Rosebud's little blizzard. At Gadshill, Falstaff and his companions scurry through a wood, their white robes soon contrasting with the roguish black of Hal and Poins. Throughout the film, Falstaff's bristling white hair is a token of his age and moral goodness. Colour would give too great a degree of glamour and warmth to Henry's austere castle, just as it would overemphasise the spectacular quality of the Battle of Shrewsbury.

This clash of armies near the Welsh border is a masterly re-creation of medieval war. Welles uses a windswept plain, with the sun high in the sky and friendly clouds contrasting with the coal-black cloak of Worcester as he listens to the royal proposal of a duel between Hal and Hotspur. When Worcester gallops back with Vernon to the rebel army, the camera descends behind a mass of pikemen, their weapons erect in defiance.

The clumsiness of the engagement affords much visual wit: men in heavy armour being winched on to their horses, Falstaff waving the infantry into battle with jerky sweeps of his sword, his bulk pronounced by a massive breastplate. Welles uses low-angle shots to emphasise the speed and urgency of the early fighting, and soldiers hurtle in agony across the glaring sky. Mist and smoke confuse the issue, and the battle becomes a series of personal clashes. There is a palpable force behind each wild swing of a ball and chain; men grunt with the sheer effort of surviving. Heads smack fatally against the ground. But the sweeping cavalry charges degenerate by degrees into a heavy violence as men and

Falstaff and Hal with the King's forces at Shrewsbury.

horses tire and the battlefield becomes a quagmire. Figures writhe and scrabble in a Flanders mudbath, their limbs jerking like Harryhausen's prehistoric monsters. They seem to be claimed by the mud— to belong to it. Falstaff hides prudently in the bushes ("Discretion is the better part of valour," Shakespeare has him say in *Henry IV, Pt 1*) and is on hand when Hotspur and the Prince come face to face. As the rivals fight, Falstaff revels vicariously in the cut and thrust, lunging so sharply at one point that he tumbles head over heels. But Percy's death brings the entertainment to a close ("O, Harry! Thou hast robbed me of my youth."). This coda, like the best scenes in *Chimes at Midnight,* has a grave and intimate quality; withdrawn, however, briefly, from the flurry of life.

Falstaff's vivid personality runs like a fugue through five of Shakespeare's plays. Welles's achievement is to have condensed and intensified this tragedy (as Verdi did with *Othello*) while in no way diminishing Shakespeare's vision. There is as noble a sense of catharsis at the end of *Chimes at Midnight* as there is at the death of Othello or Macbeth. For Falstaff, "a silhouette against the sky of all time,"[28] as Welles has termed him, comes closer than any other figure to expressing all that Welles holds good and true and dear.

The Battle of Shrewsbury in CHIMES AT MIDNIGHT. Above, the clash between cavalry and infantry. Below, the vivid personal quality of the fighting.

Fernando Rey as Worcester and Marina Vlady as Kate in a scene cut from the finished film.

THE IMMORTAL STORY

"People tend to think that my first preoccupation is with the simple plastic effects of the cinema. But to me they all come out of an interior rhythm, which is like the shape of music or the shape of poetry. I don't go around like a collector picking up beautiful images and putting them together"—ORSON WELLES[28]

PLOT OUTLINE—At the turn of the century, in Macao, there lives a wealthy merchant, Mr. Clay. His clerk, Elishama Levinsky, a Polish *émigré*, keeps his master company in the huge mansion Clay has wrested from a former partner, Ducrot. One evening Clay and this clerk discuss the legend of a rich old man who offered a sailor five guineas if he would sleep with his beautiful wife and make her with child in his stead. In spite of Levinsky's assertion that such a thing has never really happened, Clay is resolved to see the story enacted. The clerk is despatched to find a girl to fit the role. He approaches Virginie, whose father was none other than Ducrot, the partner driven to bankruptcy and suicide by Clay. Convinced by Levinsky that this charade will be the death of Mr. Clay, Virginie agrees to participate—for three hundred guineas. A sailor, Paul, is also found, and accompanies Clay and Levinsky back to the mansion. But the sailor has been shipwrecked for over a year, and when he sees Virginie he falls in love with her. Paul tells the clerk that no one will ever believe his tale and that he will never divulge it. At dawn, the lovers go their separate ways, and Clay lies dead in his chair on the verandah.

LIKE CHIMES AT MIDNIGHT, this film presents the tragedy and

Orson Welles as Mr. Clay in THE IMMORTAL STORY.

impotence of old age. The tone, however, is different. *The Immortal Story* is a meditation, drained of the sound and fury that dominate Welles's other works. It is based, quite faithfully, on Karen Blixen's short story. Welles has always worshipped this Danish writer (whose pen name was Isak Dinesen). "I spent four years writing a love letter to her and she died before I finished the letter. And I went to Denmark to see her, and I stayed three days, and I didn't have the nerve to go and see her."[26]

The Immortal Story is loved by some, scorned by others. It is true that in many prints the colours are overheated, even garish; that the drama lacks the humorous relief of Welles's earlier films; and that Welles's conception of Mr. Clay, all baleful looks and drooping moustache, is sometimes too static and banal. Against these objections, however, must be set the economy of the film—the atmosphere of Macao communicated in a few lively, richly detailed shots—and the grave, relentless rhythm of the narrative. Welles has said that "All the great technicians are dead or dying,"[50] and this explains his more restrained and less agile camera style. But in *The Immortal Story* this serenity is ideally fitted to the story. It is as if Kurosawa had set aside his dazzling fluency and opted for the tranquil pattern of Ozu's vision.

On one level the theme deals with the impossibility of making a story come true and on another, less striking but more poignant level it dwells on the essential loneliness of each human individual. Welles is attracted by the inexorable *motifs* that govern life, and the behaviour of all four characters in *The Immortal Story,* set in Macao (but in Canton in Miss Blixen's original), is distinguished by an almost Buddhist resignation. Their movements are slow, hypnotic, inevitable. Clay's life has been ordered according to a strict and ruthless plan. "The idea of friendliness had never entered his scheme of life," says Welles offscreen. His reason for arranging the encounter between Virginie and the sailor is to win an heir for his million dollar fortune. He knows that he is doomed, but his gold is "proof against dissolution," and as the clerk says, "Now he may think that the pursuit of a story is even more interesting than the pursuit of money." But Clay underestimates the players he calls to the stage for this elaborate diversion. Levinsky knows the sailor's story; Virginie recognises it at once, like a Masonic sign; and the blond Paul soon realises the part he must play. They know the rules of the game. For Clay the confrontation

Clay enters his mansion in Macao.

with illusion is too much; the story envelops him. In the words of the story, "His triumph had aged him, in a few hours his hair seemed to have grown whiter." As he sits on the verandah in the rising dawn, he mutters to Levinsky, "It's all nothing but a story, my story . . ." And of course it is Levinsky who has told Virginie apropos of the tapestry she has just woven, "Sometimes the line in the pattern goes differently to what you expect." Instead of remaining outside the legend, Clay has, like Faust, challenged its progress and been consumed.

★   ★   ★

Houses have a particular importance in Welles's films. Like Xanadu, like the Amberson mansion or Arkadin's castle, Clay's villa is both a physical expression of his life style and a cheerless, twilight zone to which he is irretrievably drawn. The secure bars that repel the outside world recall the wire fence surrounding Xanadu, and indeed the parallel with *Citizen Kane* is clear, not just because Welles plays both men. Their names, Kane and Clay, have an equally hard, monosyllabic resonance. Both men assert their will to the point that they treat those around them like puppets. "You move at my bidding," Clay tells Paul and Virginie. "Two young, strong, and lusty jumping-jacks in this old hand of mine." Here are the same mirrors that throw back countless hollow images of the dying master. Kane in his wheelchair is made up, almost mummified, in the same fashion as Clay is in his throne-like chairs. The paperweight that reminds Kane of "Rosebud" has its echo in the shell that the sailor leaves for Virginie. As the huge conch oscillates gently on the floor of the verandah, after falling from Clay's lifeless fingers, the camera dwells on it inquiringly. The shell, like Kane's paperweight, is a distillation of those hopes of paradise fostered by the mighty. "I have heard it before, long ago, but where?" asks the clerk, as he holds the conch to his ear. The sailor has gone, Clay has gone, and Levinsky is left, unable to fathom the ideal that has taunted his master.

In some respects, *The Immortal Story* is a sequel to *Citizen Kane*, for Clay lives just a little longer than Kane. Wives, mistresses, relatives—all, if any, have deserted him. The sleepless nights are spent in his upstairs room, where with bloodshot eyes he listens in a trance-like reverie to Levinsky's patient reading of the accounts. Racked by gout, he takes his dinner silent and morose. Clay is cynical, but when he gives voice to that cynicism his words are deliberately blurred as though such mundane comments had no business in this dreamlike state.

Levinsky, the wandering Jew, is as lonely as his master. Centuries

Levinsky (Roger Coggio) puts his proposal to Virginie (Jeanne Moreau).

of persecution and pogroms weigh on his shoulders. But in his un-ostentatious way, Levinsky proves to be the most durable character in the film, as hard to crush as the insect with which Welles and Miss Dinesen compare him. "He used his talents," says the story, "to fan and stir up the fire of ambition and greed in people round him. He particularly fanned the fire of Mr. Clay's ambition and greed, and watched it with an attentive eye." He is indispensable to Clay, and he remains by instinct outside the bounds of the story. Thus, like Pete Menzies in *Touch of Evil,* his entire *raison d'être* seems to be concentrated in the ordering of Clay's downfall. The scene is set to the last detail and when his master is dead, Levinsky's function and physical presence seem diminished. He carries the little parchment roll with its minute quotation from *Isaiah* like a talisman. Where Clay is a realist ("I hate prophecies" and "You should only record what has already happened in a story"), Levinsky keeps himself alive with the prophet's hope for the future. "Strengthen ye the weak knees . . . For in the wilderness shall waters break out." Nevertheless, his passive bearing suggests that he knows it is futile to try to change the course of destiny.

Attentive without being obsequious, the clerk only retires when the night is far advanced. "But there were things not yet to be re-counted," breathes Welles offscreen, "that moved like big deep-water fish in the depths of his dark mind." He walks home to his small apart-ment and is seen at the window, a frail figure sheltered by his light from the invading darkness. Levinsky's exile from society is less dramatically expressed than Clay's, but when he talks to Virginie of the unexpected pattern of life, one can guess that he is thinking of his own experience in Poland. As he speaks the film's final line, "I have heard it before, long ago, but where?" he sheds some immortal quality; he is like the cloaked man lurking in the cellar of the subconscious, as painted by Jung; or the *Alma,* the soul image of Clay, who lives on after the monster himself has passed away.

But Virginie, not the clerk, becomes the instrument of Clay's nemesis. At the very beginning of the film, his past is tersely, savagely recalled by a gaggle of merchants in the street, Fernando Rey confiding like one of Macbeth's witches the story of Clay's ruthless treatment of a former partner, Louis Ducrot (Virginie's father). Ducrot had been expelled from his own villa; he killed himself. Thus, for Virginie, the arrangement proposed by Levinsky is more than just a one-night stand. She terms it, "a comedy with the Devil." She grips the bars of the gate leading to Clay's house—the house where she grew up—and the concept of revenge takes shape in her mind. Swayed by Levinsky's assurance that, one way or another, Clay's scheme "will be the end of him," she raises her price to three hundred guineas (the very sum, Isak Dinesen tells us, that Ducrot owed Clay), and embarks on the affair. Levinsky, sensing her hesitation as she enters her father's old bedroom, is at pains to bolster her confidence. "Mr. Clay's total will come out wrong and be worth nothing," he says. "He goes about things the wrong way. You can't make a story *invented* actually happen." Vir-ginie remembers her father's dying wish that she should never again look on Clay's face. She sees the night's work as a final judgement, a settlement of accounts however high the price.

But for Virginie the price of pretence is traumatic, nothing less than the re-living of her first night of love. The sailor takes her for seventeen years of age, and toys reverently with the innocence of her name. She, the mistress of Macao, who has told the clerk previously that in comedies people only pretend to fall in love and do things, finds herself in the grip of illusion, forced to accept the sailor as the reincarnation of her lost lover, so much so that at the peak of her ecstasy she gasps, "Don't you feel the earthquake?" recalling her earlier words to Levinsky about her first night in Japan. In the dawn, she emerges silently from the bedroom, and stands in a corner of the

Virginie tells Levinsky of her hatred for Clay.

Virginie stares at the mansion once owned by her father.

Virginie prepares herself for her lover.

verandah as Levinsky pronounces the farewell to Clay. Her vengeance is fulfilled, but she is once more alone with her memories and her games of Patience. Thus the film's central *motif* is the echo, the repetition of events, phrases, reactions. Welles handles this as a composer would re-statements of an opening theme; so in the film's coda, Levinsky repeats the prophecy from *Isaiah* to his dying master.

Paul, the seventeen-year-old sailor, although appearing to be no more than an ingredient of the legend, is brought to life by Welles in a handful of choice scenes—and, like Clay, Virginie, and the clerk, he is revealed as a solitary creature. Chaste and twelve months' ship-wrecked, he reacts suspiciously to Clay's proposal. Shy of his unkempt appearance, he declines to ride in the merchant's Victoria, preferring to lope easily alongside the carriage, his hand stretched out to touch the mudguard. Thus he is attached to his new master like a possession; but his athletic stride suggests the gathering momentum of a story that is already moving out of Clay's control. As he eats his dinner in the villa, he is bathed in a golden aura of light, setting him apart from his surroundings and endowing him with divine stature. He tells Clay that his father had died six months before he was born, thus emphasis-

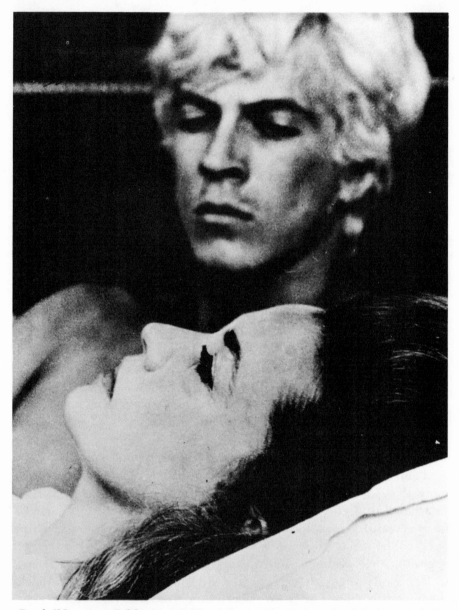

Paul (Norman Eshley) and Virginie in THE IMMORTAL STORY.

ing the isolation of his character in the drama. There is something uncanny about the way in which he tells Clay he knows there is a lady awaiting him. It is as though he had participated in this legend before, that—like Terence Stamp's Visitor in *Teorema*—he were unaware of the rejuvenation he can inspire in women; yet at the same time he is an accomplice to the scheme. In the bedroom sequences, the sailor is observed, like Virginie, in large close-ups. He is deceived by his "bride's" age and beauty, but even in the moment of falling in love with Virginie, he is denied his share in a real romance, for Virginie sees him only as the reincarnation of her first lover. When Paul leaves the room in the morning, and sees Clay in his chair on the verandah, he is still perplexed. "Who would believe it if I told it?" he asks the clerk "I would not tell it for one hundred times five guineas." He leaves his shell as a memento of his presence.

★ ★ ★

Welles has carefully designed *The Immortal Story* so as to reinforce the feeling of death and decay. The ember red and orange colours that

Virginie and her game of Patience.

predominate within the merchant's mansion suggest the glow of a dying fire. Clay is almost invariably photographed sitting down, imprisoned in huge wing and basket chairs. Ensconced in his Victoria in black cloak and silk top-hat, he is borne swiftly through the streets as if on a bier. Even on the verandah, where he slumps through the long night, Clay looks enclosed. There is a discreet wire grille surrounding one end of the balcony. Farther along, away from Clay's chair, there are the gardens, trees and sky—a landscaped freedom beyond interpretation by Clay. The plangent notes of Erik Satie's piano music underscore the melancholy inevitability of the tale. But while Clay is seen in sharp, unrelenting focus, the lovers and their fantasy are shot in a gauzy, dream-like idiom, with rose-pink tones suffusing each composition and erasing the lines from Virginie's face and neck. The old man tries to interrupt the idyll, bursting in as the sailor talks to Virginie; but Clay's bulk is merely glimpsed, like an evil presence kept at bay by the defiant tenderness and fragility of the lovers' mood. The final image of the film—Levinsky's listening to the shell—fades to a delicate pink blankness. The story, or rather illusion, has triumphed.

WELLES THE ACTOR

"Since I was twenty, nobody
has ever offered me a role corresponding to my age"—
ORSON WELLES IN 1962[27]

WELLES'S FIRST APPEARANCE on a public stage was at the age
of sixteen in *The Jew Suss* at Dublin's Gate Theatre. Since then he has
acted in over fifty plays and more than sixty films. More often than
not he has appeared in minor screen parts in order—like Vittorio
De Sica—to raise money for his own projects ("I come as a good soldier,"
he says). Today he is an international star, but he has made few
important appearances outside his own work. But his Jonathan Wilk
in Fleischer's *Compulsion* was a memorable cameo. With a well-padded
paunch, wide-bottomed trousers, and shirt-sleeved arms dangling at
his sides, he managed to convert his twelve-minute appeal for clemency
in the Leopold-Loeb murder case reconstruction into a definitive
argument against capital punishment.

"Film acting is a fascinating mystery," he said a few years ago.
"The camera seems to form its own opinions, it likes some actors and
gives others a cold, blank stare."[34] Welles himself has that ineffable
gift of magnetism; the eye is always drawn to him when he is on the
screen. Of course his immense frame and commanding voice help him
to sustain even the most exhausting roles, and one immediately recalls
him as Rochester in Robert Stevenson's version of *Jane Eyre,* and his
spectacular entry when Jane accidentally frightens his horse in the mist.
With his sweeping cloak, and a Dobermann Pinscher forever at his
heels, he fulfills the book's description of him as "proud, satanic, and
harsh." As in *Citizen Kane,* he displays an extraordinary facility for
projecting himself beyond his years into the character of a middle-aged
man. Rochester, too, is an equivocal man like so many of Welles's own
heroes, arousing the same mixture of irritation and sympathy as Georgie
Minafer, Othello and Quinlan. The film has several Wellesian touches
—the light that winks out among the gloomy towers like the light in

Welles as Rochester (left) in JANE EYRE, with Joan Fontaine.

Kane's bedroom at Xanadu; the portentous chords of Herrmann's music; the use of shadows everywhere.

Just before *Jane Eyre* Welles had played Colonel Haki in an adaptation of Eric Ambler's *Journey into Fear,* some of which he directed before his relations with RKO finally disintegrated. Everett Sloane has summed up the situation: "The RKO people were so angry with Orson about the film he had taken to Brazil . . . they assigned the direction to Norman Foster. We did all Orson's scenes first and he directed them, then Norman did the rest of it. I think it retains much of Orson's original conception of the picture."[126]

PLOT OUTLINE—Howard Graham (Joseph Cotten) is an American engineer surveying Turkish ships preparatory to their being modernised with new guns and armour. He has completed his work and is about to return to America with his wife Stephanie (Ruth Warrick). The Nazis try to kill him so as to delay the modernisation. At an Istanbul café Graham narrowly escapes a bullet that kills another man instead. Colonel Haki, head of the Turkish secret service, persuades

Graham to slip aboard a Greek ship bound for Batum and assures him that he will escort Mrs. Graham to the same town by train. On board the ship, Graham is trapped by Moeller, the head Nazi agent, under the guise of a quiet old professor. He is eventually forced to agree to the latter's terms, but manages to escape at Batum, only to find that Moeller and his thugs have reached his wife's hotel first. Graham kills the Nazi gunman after a chase along a narrow window ledge. Colonel Haki has already disposed of Moeller and the husband and wife can make their way home in peace.

Welles's touch is apparent in scenes other than his own (and to me he will only admit, tactfully, that he "was on the set for about the first third of the shooting"†). The opening crane shot creeps up the crumbling plaster of a boarding house in Istanbul, and then probes through the window of a darkened room, where an assassin checks his weapon and combs his greasy hair to the nerve-wracking accompaniment of a scratched record in which the gramophone needle has stuck (the man is played by Jack Moss, Welles's agent at the time). Then there is the pursuit along the window ledge at the end, with the people on the pavement viewed from a vertiginous angle. Joseph Cotten collaborated with Welles on the scenario, and some of the inane humour that enlivens the scenes on board the cargo boat suggests his influence. Viewed now, *Journey into Fear* curiously fails to fire the imagination. Few sequences contain the genuine suspense of Eric Ambler's original novel. It is only Welles who brings a touch of arrogance and vigour to the proceedings, whether enveloping Graham in his bear-like embrace, or staggering back with a mighty crash through one of the windows of the hotel at Batum after being wounded by a Nazi agent. There is a legend, Graham is told, that Haki can consume two bottles of whisky without getting drunk. This concept of a "walking legend" reminds one of Arkadin and Harry Lime.

Haki, with his Astrakhan hat, hooked nose, bushy eyebrows, and passion for Turkish cigarettes, set the fashion for Welles's subsequent roles. The image of a man of controlled, sinister power can be applied to the majority of his parts, from Rochester to van Horn in *Ten Days' Wonder*. It colours his appearance as the scheming and unscrupulous Cesare Borgia in *Prince of Foxes,* a costume drama of the Renaissance shot at monstrous expense in Italy by Twentieth-Century-Fox. And it predominates in his portrayal of the Eighteenth century charlatan, Cagliostro, in *Black Magic,* a performance that led Margaret Hinxman to describe his career in other directors' films as resembling that of "a kind of intellectual Boris Karloff." Salka Viertel had asked Welles a

Welles as Colonel Haki in JOURNEY INTO FEAR.

few years earlier to play Cagliostro opposite Greta Garbo, and Welles still regrets that the plan never materialised.

The Third Man, however, added a new dimension to Welles's playing. The drug trafficker Harry Lime is on screen for only a few minutes, yet his malignant personality stains every sequence. "I hate Harry Lime: he has no passion; he is cold; he is Lucifer, the fallen angel."[25] Yet what are any of Welles's heroes—bar Falstaff—if not satanic? Lime has a haunting, mocking smile hovering on his chalky face that first appears when a cat discovers his hiding-place and the light of a passing vehicle picks him out in a doorway, black hat and black coat imparting to him a kind of Feuillade-esque malevolence. The final chase through the sewers seems to have been directed by Welles, to judge from the similar sequence in *The Trial* when K flees from Titorelli's studio. As in *Journey into Fear*, one cannot help suspecting that Welles may have had a hand in certain vital scenes. "The whole story, the conception and the setting, were really Korda's. He just got Greene to write it—and I wrote my own part."[30] For the first time outside his own films, Welles was able to show just how skilful and restrained an actor he could be. His conversation with Joseph

Cotten in the Prater wheel high above the Viennese streets is a masterpiece of timing, and every gesture, every casual remark is fraught with
menace and ambiguity.

Two years later, Welles made an appearance as himself in Hilton
Edwards's short film, *Return to Glennascaul,* shot during the filming
of *Othello* in Dublin. He narrates a ghost story told him by a man
to whom he had given a lift in the country, "one spooky Irish midnight." Welles deceives neither himself nor the audience as to the
degree of truth in the tale, but his enlivening presence and an occasional moment of apprehension give it the intimacy of a shared joke.
Again, one has the feeling that the hand of the master may have chosen
a camera angle here, or set an extra shadow there. The eerie atmosphere
of the story was authentic enough, for Hilton Edwards did not have
a chance to start shooting until midnight in a disused house outside
Dublin, since he was occupied twelve hours a day with theatre re-
hearsals.

But Welles's other roles have not been written or devised to any-

*Welles as Harry Lime talks to his old friend Joseph Cotten (Holly
Martins in this film) in the Prater wheel above Vienna.*

Welles in John Guillermin's HOUSE OF CARDS.

Welles as the TV reporter in THE ROOTS OF HEAVEN.

Welles talking with John Huston on the set of MOBY DICK.

where approaching his own high standards. The irascible American television reporter in John Huston's *The Roots of Heaven,* the disgruntled, toffee-nosed ferry-boat captain in *Ferry to Hong Kong,* the rather naïve, genial film magnate in *Trouble in the Glen,* and the slumbrous Saul, complete with auburn wig and bloodshot eyes, of *David and Goliath,* comprise a grotesque gallery of characters that are almost deliberately not drawn in depth. His portrayal of the ambitious, overblown plantation owner, Will Varner, in Martin Ritt's *The Long Hot Summer* carries more conviction and his mastery of the Deep South accent is skilful, while his vignette as Father Mapple in *Moby Dick* is more complimentary to his oratory than to his capacity as an actor.

In *A Man for All Seasons* he is seen as Wolsey, squatting heavily in a scarlet robe and a scarlet cap in a scarlet room. In *Catch-22* he alights from a plane as General Dreedle, cigar-chewing and full of mocking asides. And in *Ten Days' Wonder* he has a role worthy of his talents at last, as Theo van Horn, a kind of Arkadin in retirement in Alsace, bearded and authoritative in a *ménage* that seems forever locked in the dress and attitudes of the Twenties.

Yet nothing Welles does on the screen is without interest, and one

Welles (as Cardinal Wolsey) and Paul Scofield listen to director Fred Zinnemann on A MAN FOR ALL SEASONS.

must after all take into account his ten brilliant performances in his own work when judging his gifts as an actor. Apart from him, only Sjöström and von Stroheim have been able to direct themselves consistently with any measure of success (Olivier in his Shakespearian films had an advantage, surely, in that the parts were familiar to him on the stage before he acted them out for the screen).

CONCLUSION

"A film is a dream. A dream
that is perhaps vulgar, stupid,
dull and shapeless; it is perhaps a nightmare. But a
dream is never an illusion.
—ORSON WELLES[20]

"Orson Welles is a kind of
giant with a childlike face, a
tree filled with birds and
shadows, a dog who has
snapped his chain and lies in
the flowerbeds, an active
idler, a wise fool, isolation
surrounded by humanity, a
student who dozes in class, a
strategist who pretends to be
drunk when he wants to be
left in peace"—JEAN COC-
TEAU[41]

WELLES'S WORK—HIS THEMES, HIS STYLE—has an organic
unity, despite its terrible birthpangs, with the long periods of creative
inactivity, the patently harmful interventions by his sponsors and the
subsequent mishandling of the montage. No one has quite the same
outlook on life, but certainly Elia Kazan, Nicholas Ray, Joseph Losey,
Otto Preminger, Samuel Fuller, Robert Wise (who helped to edit
Welles's first two films), Stanley Kubrick, Leopoldo Torre-Nilsson,
Louis Malle, Roman Polanski, and Robert Aldrich owe an incalculable
debt to Welles's art.

With Welles more than with most directors, *le style c'est l'homme*.
It is a fascinating style, opportunist to a degree and yet strongly sug-
gestive of minute artifice and preparation. When I asked Welles if he
planned every shot in his shooting scripts, he replied: "I plan every
shot then throw all the plans out. The images have to be discovered
in the course of work or else they are cold and lack life."*

One point that should be made quite plain when examining
Welles's style is that it spurns realism. "I am passionately fond of films
that, while turning their back on fiction, are not of the 'Here's the

truth, here is life etc.' school, but are full of opinions, expressing the personality and ideas of their creators."[23] One calls to mind the Neapolitan films of De Sica, so highly regarded by Welles. And again: "Carné is not a realist, you know, but he transfigures reality in his style. What is interesting is Carné's style and not the reality he depicts."[68] Instead, Welles creates his own environment, a world of shadows and bright light. He is like a sorcerer conjuring up images that seem to have strayed from some extravagant nightmare. A flash of his genius lights up the landscape so that for an instant everything, even the souls of his characters, is laid bare. He is frequently criticised for using dazzling effects to display his virtuosity rather than to aid the plot or the characters thereby. But what such criticism fails to take into account is that his breathtaking imagination repeatedly manages to find the right visual parallel for an emotional condition (thus the parakeet in *Citizen Kane;* the subterranean passage through which Joseph K flees the children in *The Trial;* the hall of mirrors at the end of *The Lady from Shanghai* that multiplies and distorts the features of Elsa and Arthur Bannister).

As John Houseman, his early associate at the Mercury Theatre and himself a film producer, has said: "Welles is at heart a magician whose particular talent lies not so much in his creative imagination (which is considerable) as in his proven ability to stretch the familiar elements of theatrical effect far beyond their normal point of tension."[51] His is a world of semi-darkness that hatches evil deeds and cloaks them with an air of ghostly unreality. Conversely, light is more vital to him than to other directors. Often, as in a fifth of *The Trial,* he resorts to reflected light that lends a grey, uncertain effect to a scene. He also makes much use, as Bazin has noted, of the upward-thrown light, so that faces are given a slightly demoniac look; whereas light thrown downwards, as in Dreyer, for instance, denotes a spiritual atmosphere. The angled shot also has an essential place in Welles's technique. The upward tilt increases the stature of a Kane, an Arkadin, or a Quinlan; the leaning shot conveys the idea of an unbalanced situation or view of the world.

All these, and other effects, are witness to Welles's baroque style. In his own words, "I do try to keep the screen as rich as possible, because I never forget that the film itself is a dead thing, and for me, at least, the illusion of life fades very quickly when the texture is thin."[34] His camera is rarely still (a notable exception is the famous kitchen scene in *The Magnificent Ambersons*) ; mobility is imperative. Always in a Welles film, one feels that the camera sees, subjectively, through the eye of a human being. Thus his fondness for the wide-angle lens, surprisingly neglected by so many other directors. Nearly all of *Touch of Evil, The Trial* and *Don Quixote* are shot in 18.5mm.

The montage is even more crucial. "No one can pretend to be a good film director unless he does his own editing," says Welles,[142] and he works like a Titan on this aspect of his films. "I'm a fast director, slow editor. I make three days' editing for one day's shooting."[26] *Citizen Kane* preoccupied him at the cutting table for several months, six days a week; he devoted eighteen hours or more a day to the editing of *The Trial* during the autumn of 1962; and the battle sequence in *Chimes at Midnight* took two and a half weeks to assemble. "For my style, for my vision of the cinema, montage is not an aspect, it is *the* aspect . . . the images themselves are not sufficient; they are very important, but they are only images. The essential thing is the duration of each image, and what follows each image . . . I search for an exact rhythm between one frame and the next. It's a question of ear: the editing is the moment when the film comes to terms with the hearing. . . . You'll notice that in the course of these past years, the films that I have made are mostly in short shots, because I have less money and the style of the short shot is more economical."[23] In other words, his style constantly reflects his anxiety to express the maximum possible in the minimum of screen time; his *penchant* for deep-focus photography symbolises this desire. A mediocre film like *The Stranger* is often lifted above its station by the suppleness and inventiveness of the lighting, camera movement, and editing. It is, finally, this ability to transcend even the meanest material that will always distinguish anything Welles does in the cinema.

Nearly all his work reveals an uncanny knowledge of sound effects. Like Bresson, Chaplin, and Grémillon, Welles attaches great importance to the soundtrack. Not merely to the music—although his discovery of Bernard Herrmann (who worked on several of Welles's radio shows) helped Hitchcock enormously later, but also to the actual mixing and overlapping of sounds. His experience as a broadcaster gave him an unparalleled ear: the soundtrack of *The Trial,* with pieces of Albinoni played backwards and integrated at times with jazz, the screaming of children or a hammering of typewriters, is a *tour de force.* The music in *The Magnificent Ambersons* is less obtrusive but also helps the drama to shift gear from one long sequence to another. Even in the "News on the March" section of *Kane,* Welles has Thatcher's voice in the White House Committee overlapped and overruled by the snappy questions of reporters.

★   ★   ★

It is one of the most stimulating truisms about Welles that even though, like Dostoievsky and Hardy, he returns to the same basic themes, he is forever finding fresh situations and characters through which to investigate them. Ambition, jealousy, egotism and retribution are the recurring tokens of his universe. Like the Elizabethan stage that he adores so much, Welles's own screen is filled to abundance with a rich selection of characters, clowns mingling with kings and villains with innocent men.

When he was a child and felt the urge to pray to God, Welles would pray to Chaliapin instead. He used to sit on Chaliapin's lap and the big Russian would tell him, "Some day you will become a great *basso*." And among film directors Welles undoubtedly belongs to the Imperial ranks, every inch a virtuoso, unique in voice, looks, and largeness of spirit.

APPENDIX 1

Welles and Writing for the Cinema

"In my opinion the writer should have the first and last word in film-making, the only better alternative being the writer-director, but with stress on the first word."[32]

"The real film-maker is a writer. He's a director whether he writes the script or not. It's a literary process, I think. And if he writes the dialogue, all the better. If he doesn't write the dialogue, it's still the director's picture; and if the dialogue director feels that he's getting a bad deal then he should be a director or go into another line of business."[31]

APPENDIX 2

CONSIDERABLE RESEARCH HAS BEEN DEVOTED to the truth about *It's All True,* the film that Welles shot in South America in 1942. Charles Higham, Peter Bogdanovich, and Richard Wilson have all been arguing about the details of the production (although only Higham, for all his faults, has spent much space actually *describing* the extant footage).

In an interview with Kenneth Tynan in 1966, Welles commented: "All the pictures I've directed have been made within their budgets. The only exception was a documentary about South America that I started in 1942, just after I finished shooting *The Magnificent Ambersons.* I was asked to do it by the Government for no salary but with $1,000,000 to spend. But it was the studio's money, not the Government's, and the studio fired me when I'd spent $600,000, on the basis that I was throwing money away."[36] Nelson Rockefeller and Jock Whitney had persuaded him, at short notice, that the only hope of saving the situation in Latin America (in view of the war) was to undertake the project. There was no script, according to Welles.

It's All True was intended to be a normal feature-length film, consisting of various short stories, shot in Mexico and Brazil. The Brazilian episode included the Carnival of Rio (in colour) and Robert Florey, one of those who managed to see what remained of the 100,000 feet of film (not 400,000 feet as so often claimed) exposed by Welles, has said that by comparison the carnival sequences of *Black Orpheus* look the work of an amateur. The second story concerned four Brazilian fishermen who became national heroes; and the third was scripted by Robert Flaherty from an actual incident, when a bull conducted himself so bravely in the *corrida* that he was set out to pasture for the rest of his life. It was called *My Friend Bonito* and was in black-and-white.

Like Eisenstein's *Que viva Mexico!*, however, it was a true *film maudit,* and Welles's dispute with RKO in the midst of things finally thwarted the idea. "Back in Hollywood, where nobody had even heard of the samba—this was 1942—the film we were sending back looked fairly mysterious. No stars. No actors even. 'Just a lot of coloured

people,' to quote one studio executive, 'playing their drums and jumping up and down in the streets.' "[34] But the exotic and sensational
circumstances of *It's All True* should not divert the critic too much
from Welles's more thoughtful, achieved *oeuvre*.

★   ★   ★

Cervantes has long been one of Welles's favourite authors, and it
is a great pity that Welles has not, at the time of writing, released his
film version of *Don Quixote*. This film was originally designed for the
American television market and stars Francisco Reiguera and Akim
Tamiroff. Shooting continued over a period of some fifteen years and
was only completed in 1971. As one has come to expect with Welles,
he has changed the shape of several incidents and situations in the novel
(although, as with *The Trial*, the moral and the effect of his version
are similar to that of the original) ; one should bear in mind too that
Don Quixote and Sancho Panza were themselves anachronistic when
Cervantes was writing, and in the second volume people frequently
say: "Look! There are Don Quixote and Sancho Panza. We have read
the book about them!" Welles has said, "Cervantes gave them [Don
Quixote and Sancho Panza] an amusing dimension, as if they were both
characters of fiction and more real than life itself. My Don Quixote
and Sancho Panza are exactly and traditionally drawn from Cervantes
but are nonetheless contemporary."[23] The point is, as he has since
stressed, that this couple never die—they are still with us.

Thus one of the episodes in the film shows Don Quixote in a cinema,
rushing to the aid of the heroine, menaced by traitors in a spectacle,
only to split the screen (this is, of course, Welles's interpretation of
the fight with the Moors) ; in another, the "windmills" of the novel
are reincarnated in the form of a power-shovel that sucks Don Quixote
down into the mud; in yet another, he defends a bull in the ring. The
final episode apparently shows the Don and his squire surviving an
atomic cataclysm unharmed.

Welles has described the splendid ease and liberty that prevailed
during the production, attenuated though it was. He would meet his
actors and technical crew in front of his Spanish hotel each morning
and then they would set about improvising the film in the streets, in
the style of Mack Sennett.[23] Scarcely any post-synchronisation is involved, and Welles has linked the film with a commentary and dialogue
spoken by him. He also appears as himself, and when the film opens he
is seen engrossed in Cervantes's novel in a Mexican hotel: Patty Mc-
Cormack (the child in Mervyn LeRoy's *The Bad Seed*) is a young

American tourist who asks Welles what he is reading. He tries to explain the book in terms that a present-day child can grasp.

Don Quixote is the only feature film that Welles has made entirely from his own money (he had to take the part of Varner in *The Long Hot Summer* in order to pay for some of the shooting) , and every scene was filmed with an 18.5mm lens.

★ ★ ★

The Deep, filmed in Yugoslavia a couple of years ago, stars Laurence Harvey with Jeanne Moreau alongside Welles himself. "It's basically a thriller," says Welles, "taking place on a couple of small boats in the middle of the ocean." A much bigger production, probably occupying some ten weeks of shooting, is *The Other Side of the Wind,* in which Welles is currently (early 1972) engrossed. It consists of two films in one, and revolves round a film director's birthday party—a director of John Ford's generation and a Hemingway figure (he's named Jack Hannaford) . "During the party," says Welles, "you see the film he's making. It's not just about films, it's about Machuism, you know, lots of things, the whole Hemingway stuff."[26] Welles will not appear in *The Other Side of the Wind,* but Marlene Dietrich, Jeanne Moreau and, hopefully, Pierre Fresnay will, with cameo appearances by Welles fans Joseph McBride and Peter Bogdanovich, as well as by old friends like Mercedes McCambridge and Edmond O'Brien.

APPENDIX 3

THE THIRD AUDIENCE, by Orson Welles (reprinted from *Sight and Sound,* London, January-March 1954).

On the Film Industry

WHENEVER FILM STUDENTS, or film scholars, or anyone not actively concerned with the commercial world of film-making, invite someone like myself to give a lecture, they always talk about art. But we are business men. If I were a painter, I might have to starve for a while, but I would find paper or canvas or even a wall on which to express myself. Being a film-maker in the commercial world, and not in the documentary or avant-garde field, I need a million dollars to make a film. You have to be a business man to handle a million dollars. I remember sitting with Jean Cocteau and René Clair in a meeting of this sort, intensely serious, and we were regarded as being cynical because we refused to talk about anything but what films cost.

The invention of the moving picture was a moment of historic importance equivalent to the invention of movable type. Let us suppose that the business of publishing books was just beginning, and that, because the manufacture of movable type was so easy, an enormous industry had just grown up. Then suppose that only two types of books could be published: little tiny ones that very few people would read or buy, and books like "Gone with the Wind". How many books would have been published, in fact, or would even have been written, if an author, in order to get a publisher to publish what he had written, had to assume the responsibility of addressing himself to an audience of sixty million people?

There is nothing wrong with popular art; some of the greatest artists in the world have been popular artists. But the trouble with films is that they cost too much. I am now acting in a film in London, made from a short story by Somerset Maugham. Knowing him to be a writer who works at the normal speed, it should have taken him no more than four half-days to write that story, but it will take five weeks of shooting to make that same story a film. Logically, it should not take any longer, or, at the very most, twice the time it took Maugham, but with hundreds of people clanking around a great set where the camera is so heavy it takes three people to move it, a faster and more economical method of work becomes impossible. We are now all trapped by a standard of technical excellence, which we dare not fall below without being attacked by the whole system—from the distributor to the exhibitor, from the highbrow to the lowbrow critic, from everyone, in fact, except the public.

I think movies are dying, dying, dying. But I do not think they are going to stay dead for long. They are like the theatre; the theatre is dying all the time, but it never dies altogether. It is like the cycle of the seasons—it has its summer, autumn and winter. Now the movies are in the autumn of the cycle.

On the Film Public

For the first time in the history of the world, a creative artist is now given the opportunity to address sixty million people. The trouble is, it is not simply an opportunity, but an obligation—he *must* address them. The new artist goes out to Hollywood or Rome or wherever it may be, and until the industrialists grow wise to him, he may create something out of himself, something original. Then they grow wise to him, and make him feel responsible to the industry. In fact, he simply becomes a responsible man who does not like to steal from the people who are paying him.

So we have to find some ground between the experimental 16mm. avant-garde—although that medium is important—and the commercial production—which is, anyway, dying from an economic point of view. If the Eady plan were taken away from the British film industry, if government aid were removed from the French, the Italian or the Spanish industries, they would collapse. India and Japan are the only two national film industries that are paying their way. What we need, in fact, is to hold a world congress to discuss the whole economics of film-making, and to study the public.

We talk much about the public, but the fact is that the film public is *petit bourgeois*. What the big commercial film is doing is to interpret for the lower middle classes what the upper middle classes liked yesterday. That is not snobbery—I am simply using terms of social reality. Another curious thing is that this film public has no shape.

If I were to play King John at the Edinburgh Festival, I would know the shape of my public; but a film is manufactured and then shipped out to a series of halls throughout the world into which a huge and amorphous public pours. Nobody really knows anything about it. It is made up of everybody, of kings and queens and cleaners and clerks. The best thing commercially, which is the worst artistically, by and large, is the most successful; and, that being the fact, how can we be surprised if the level of films goes down and down?

The creative film-maker may well wonder where he is going to find his public. He is generally faced with two choices; he can either make straightforward commercial films, films that the public can be expected to pay to see, or he can do exactly what he wants and be supported by his government. Neither alternative, on its own, is a good one. I reject state patronage to the exclusion of all other forms, but I think it is a very serious thing when a government gives no help. America needs a B.B.C. and Britain needs a C.B.S. If the cinema is to be a stable industry, it must be economically possible for a man to produce a film without going to his government; but, on the other hand, he should be able to go to it if he wants to.

I would like a public and a film in which it is possible to exchange and communicate ideas and information. Certainly, in an educated world, there will be two hundred million people who will be bored to death by the most "difficult" film we make today, but as things stand only so many people will listen to Mozart. That is a limited public. It grows by what it feeds on. You must nourish that public, and you cannot do so with 16mm. avant-garde films, because that is too far away from the general public to be an important source of expression for the film-maker.

The biggest mistake we have made is to consider that films are primarily a form of entertainment. The film is the greatest medium since the invention of movable type for exchanging ideas and information, and it is no more at its best in light entertainment than literature is at its best in the light novel. This doesn't mean that the great public of today should be abandoned, but I think there should be other publics, smaller ones, and cosmopolitan ones, to see things forbidden by the code of Hollywood, the censors of the Vatican, and whatever the gentlemen in Britain are called. There must be a relatively free exchange of ideas. To achieve this, we have to find a way of making films—and here television may help us—by which, if two or three million people see them, we have a return for our money; which involves the creation of a true international audience, and a struggle with the mysterious national forces in the world which call themselves governments. But out of such a victory would come the raw material for a great new enterprise.

On Rome, Hollywood and Elsewhere

It is old-fashioned to blame Hollywood. We have seen Rome turn into a small Hollywood, and England try to do so and fall flat on its face. Hollywood has simply been the biggest and most productive film-making centre. It was a cosmopolitan place and it might have happened anywhere. It only happened in a suburb of Los Angeles because Cecil B. de Mille was prevented from moving on to Nevada by the snow.

The fact is that everything wrong with Hollywood is also there in Rome today. The Italian films, by the way, cost a great deal more than their publicity indicated. Rossellini is an extremely expensive director. The Italians did not make their films cheaply—it was simply that there was no way of their costing more. They should neither be praised nor blamed for this. Having always been a calligraphic people, they reacted against calligraphism after the war, and many of the results were called neo-realism by one side and bad movie-making by the other.

When I referred to England falling flat on its face, I did not mean artistically; I meant, by trying to industrialise its film business on such a scale, England is the only film industry without a tradition. They were making films in Stockholm, Budapest and Copenhagen forty years ago, but they were not making them in London. You walk into a studio in England today, and the number of people who have been in films for more than five years is hardly enough to push a camera.

On the Wide Screen

When someone asked Cocteau what he thought of the wide screen, he said: "The next poem I write, I am going to get a big sheet of paper." We must stop thinking in terms of technique. I do not think the film public deserves anything bigger or better than it has got already. Films are big enough for a while. One of the biggest distributors in England, an intelligent and talented man, recently ran in a provincial theatre the film, *The War of the Worlds;* and he installed for that week a large screen, although there was no mention of this fact in his publicity. Afterwards he conducted a poll among the audience, and not one member of it, not one person who visited the theatre during that week, knew that it was a wide screen.

On Filming Shakespeare

I am not necessarily in favour of putting Shakespeare on the screen. I do not know whether a happy marriage can exist between Shakespeare and the screen, and I certainly know that I did not succeed in making one. But in this age, there are many questions which cannot be discussed in front of sixty million people, and that is the audience a present-day film-maker is required to aim at. One method of getting away from banality is to return to our classics, and it is for this reason one sees film-makers experimenting with Shakespeare, some disastrously, and some otherwise.

Macbeth was made in twenty-three days, including one day of retakes. People who know anything at all about the business of making a film will realise that this is more than fast. My purpose in making *Macbeth* was not to make a great film—and this is unusual, because I think that every film director, even when he is making nonsense, should have as his purpose the making of a great film. I thought I was making what might be a good film, and what, if the twenty-three day shooting schedule came off, might encourage other film-makers to tackle difficult subjects at greater speed.

Unfortunately, not one critic in any part of the world chose to compliment me on the speed. They thought it a scandal that it should take only twenty-three days. Of course they were right, but I could not write to every one of them and explain that no one would give me any money for a further day's shooting. I believe that we have got to find in films an equivalent for the repertory theatre in spoken drama. The experiment in America failed because it was judged on the same level, and distributed in the same way, as the work that took four months to make. However, I am not ashamed of the limitations of the picture.

Othello took not twenty-three days but four years to make. It did not, however, take four years to shoot. Actually, its shooting period was about the normal one, but there were times when it was necessary to disband the unit, because I had to go away and act elsewhere. *Macbeth,* for better or worse, is a kind of violently sketched charcoal drawing of a great play. *Othello,* whether successful or not, is about as close to Shakespeare's play as was Verdi's opera. I think Verdi and Boito were perfectly entitled to change Shakespeare in adapting him to another art form; and, assuming that the film is an art form, I took the line that you can adapt a classic freely and vigorously for the cinema.

On Films and Television

The technical excellence of the images in that Punch and Judy set, television, is about as bad as a picture of a Chinese play, in which someone brings on a chair and tells you it's a mountain. Yet the public is sufficiently held by that. In fact, one of the hopes of the movies is television, and not just television as a means of diffusing movies. The lightness and ease of some television productions contain a lesson for film-makers to learn again. Television is an exciting thing because it is in the hands of the first generation. Films have not exhausted their technical and artistic possibilities, but the majority of movie-makers today belong to the second generation, and they are ashamed of the first generation.

It is rather as if we had just left a period of Elizabethan eloquence and entered a more cautious, lyrical and decadent period. The possibilities of the Elizabethan period were no more exhausted than the possibilities of the language were exhausted; it was just that people became afraid of the richness of the language. You can still do anything with films, and television is not a substitute for them. Eventually it may become a means of distributing them, but it will never give the director the scope that the film camera can give him. Television is an actor's medium. It is going to reduce the director to something like his position in the theatre. But the great power of the film, the use of the image as such, will always belong to the cinema.

Adapted from a lecture given by Welles at the 1953 Edinburgh Festival.

APPENDIX 4

Feature Films Made by Orson Welles

CITIZEN KANE

U.S.A. 1940/41. A Mercury Production (Orson Welles). Released by RKO. *Script*: Herman J. Mankiewicz and Orson Welles (Joseph Cotten and John Houseman also helped). *Direction*: Orson Welles. *Photography*: Gregg Toland. *Editing*: Robert Wise (and Mark Robson). *Art Direction*: Van Nest Polglase. *Associate Art Direction*: Perry Ferguson. *Music*: Bernard Herrmann. *Costumes*: Edward Stevenson. *Decors*: Darrell Silvera. *Special Effects*: Vernon L. Walker. *Sound Recording*: Bailey Fesler and James G. Stewart. *Newsreel Narrated by*: William Alland. 119 minutes.

CAST. Joseph Cotten (*Jedediah Leland*), Dorothy Comingore (*Susan Alexander*), Agnes Moorehead (*Kane's mother*), Ruth Warrick (*Emily*), Ray Collins (*Jim Gettys*), Erskine Sanford (*Carter*), Everett Sloane (*Bernstein*), William Alland (*Thompson, the reporter*), Paul Stewart (*Raymond*), George Coulouris (*Thatcher*), Fortunio Bonanova (*Matisti*), Gus Schilling (*Head waiter*), Philip Van Zandt (*Rawlston*), Richard Baer (*Hillman*), Joan Blair (*Georgia*), Georgia Backus (*Miss Anderson*), Harry Shannon (*Kane's father*), Alan Ladd (*Reporter*), Sonny Bupp (*Kane's son*), Buddy Swan (*Kane at the age of eight*), Orson Welles (*Charles Foster Kane*), with Richard Wilson, Charles Bennett, Edith Evanson, Louise Currie, Arthur O'Connell, Milt Kibbee, Richard Barr.

Shot from July 30 to October 23, 1940, in RKO Studios, Hollywood. Premiered May 1, 1941 (New York) and May 8, 1941 (Hollywood).

THE MAGNIFICENT AMBERSONS

U.S.A. 1942. A Mercury Production (Orson Welles). Released by

RKO. *Script*: Orson Welles, from the novel by Booth Tarkington. *Direction*: Orson Welles. *Photography*: Stanley Cortez. *Editing*: Robert Wise and Mark Robson. *Art Direction*: Mark Lee Kirk. *Set Dresser*: Al Fields. *Music*: Bernard Herrmann (and Roy Webb). *Special Effects*: Vernon L. Walker. *Costumes*: Edward Stevenson. *Sound Recording*: Bailey Fesler and James G. Stewart. *Narration*: Orson Welles. *Assistant Director*: Freddie Fleck. 88 minutes.

CAST. Tim Holt (*George Minafer Amberson*), Joseph Cotten (*Eugene Morgan*), Dolores Costello (*Isabel Amberson*), Anne Baxter (*Lucy Morgan*), Agnes Moorehead (*Fanny Minafer*), Ray Collins (*Uncle Jack Amberson*), Erskine Sanford (*Roger Bronson*), Richard Bennett (*Major Amberson*), Don Dillaway (*Wilbur Minafer*), J. Louis Johnson (*Sam*), Charles Phipps (*Uncle John*), with Georgia Backus, Gus Schilling.

Shot from October 28, 1941 to January 22, 1942, in RKO Studios, Hollywood. Premiered August 13, 1942.

THE STRANGER

U.S.A. 1946. Haig Corporation/An International Pictures Production (S. P. Eagle). Released by RKO, then by United Artists. *Original Story*: Victor Trivas and Decla Dunning. *Screenplay*: Anthony Veiller (also Orson Welles, John Huston). *Direction*: Orson Welles. *Photography*: Russell Metty. *Editing*: Ernest Nims. *Production Design*: Perry Ferguson. *Music*: Bronislaw Kaper. *Costumes*: Michael Woulfe. *Assistant Director*: Jack Voglin. 95 minutes.

CAST. Orson Welles (*Franz Kindler/Charles Rankin*), Loretta Young (*Mary Longstreet*), Edward G. Robinson (*Inspector Wilson*), Philip Merivale (*Judge Longstreet*), Richard Long (*Noah Longstreet*), Byron Keith (*Dr. Lawrence*), Billy House (*Mr. Potter*), Martha Wentworth (*Sarah*), Konstantin Shayne (*Konrad Meinike*), Theodore Gottlieb (*Farbright*), Pietro Sosso (*Mr. Peabody*), Erskine Sanford (*Guest at party*).

Shot in Hollywood in 1945 in RKO Studios.

THE LADY FROM SHANGHAI

U.S.A. 1946/48. Produced and released by Columbia. *Script*: Orson Welles, from the novel *If I Die Before I Wake*, by Sherwood King. *Direction*: Orson Welles. *Photography*: Charles Lawton, Jr. *Editing*: Viola Lawrence. *Art Direction*: Stephen Goosson and Sturges Carne. *Set Decoration*: Wilbur Menefee and Herman Schoenbrun. *Music*: Heinz Roemheld. *Song*: "Please Don't Kiss Me," by Roberts and Fisher.

Special Effects: Lawrence Butler (*mirror maze*). *Costumes*: Jean Louis. *Sound*: Lodge Cunningham. *Camera Operator*: Irving Klein. *Assistant Director*: Sam Nelson. *Associate Producers*: Richard Wilson and William Castle. 86 minutes.

CAST. Orson Welles (*Michael O'Hara*), Rita Hayworth (*Elsa Bannister*), Everett Sloane (*Arthur Bannister*), Glenn Anders (*Grisby*), Ted de Corsia (*Sidney Broom*), Gus Schilling (*Goldie*), Erskine Sanford (*The Judge*), Louis Merrill (*Jake*), Harry Shannon (*Taxi driver*), Evelyn Ellis (*Bessie*), Wong Show Ching (*Li*), Sam Nelson (*The Captain*), Carl Frank (*District Attorney*), Richard Wilson (*D.A.'s assistant*).

Shot in late 1946 in Columbia Studios, Hollywood, and in Mexico and San Francisco on location.

MACBETH

U.S.A. 1948. A Mercury Production (Orson Welles). Released by Republic. *Script*: Orson Welles, from the play by William Shakespeare. *Direction*: Orson Welles. *Photography*: John L. Russell. *Editing*: Louis Lindsay. *Art Direction*: Fred Ritter. *Sets*: John McCarthy Jr. and James Redd. *Music*: Jacques Ibert. *Music Conducted by*: Efrem Kurtz. *Costumes*: Orson Welles and Fred Ritter (men) and Adele Palmer (women). *Special Effects*: Howard and Theodore Lydecker. *Sound*: John Stransky Jr. and Garry Harris. *Dialogue Director*: William Alland. *Hair Styles*: Peggy Gray. *Second Unit Direction*: William Bradford. *Make-up*: Bob Mark. *Assistant Director*: Jack Lacey. *Optical Effects*: Consolidated Film Industries. *Producer*: Charles K. Feldman. 86 minutes.

CAST. Orson Welles (*Macbeth*), Jeanette Nolan (*Lady Macbeth*), Dan O'Herlihy (*Macduff*), Roddy McDowall (*Malcolm*), Edgar Barrier (*Banquo*), Alan Napier (*A Holy Father*), Erskine Sanford (*Duncan*), John Dierkes (*Ross*), Keene Curtis (*Lennox*), Peggy Webber (*Lady Macduff*), Lurene Tuttle (voice only), Brainerd Duffield, and Peggy Webber (voice only) (*The Three Witches*), Lurene Tuttle (*Gentlewoman*), Christopher Welles (*Macduff's son*), Morgan Farley (*Doctor*), George Chirello (*Seyton*), Lionel Braham (*Siward*), Jerry Farber (*Fleance*), Archie Heugly (*Young Siward*), Gus Schilling (*Porter*), Brainerd Duffield (*First Murderer*), Robert Alan (*Second Murderer*).

Shot in twenty-three days (after four months of rehearsal) in Republic Studios, Hollywood.

OTHELLO

Morocco. 1951. A Mercury Production (Orson Welles). Released by Films Marceau and United Artists. *Script*: Orson Welles, from the play by William Shakespeare. *Direction*: Orson Welles. *Photography*: Anchise Brizzi, G. R. Aldo, George Fanto, with Obadan Troiani, Roberto Fusi. *Editing*: Jean Sacha, with Renzo Lucidi, John Shepridge. *Art Direction*: Alexandre Trauner. *Music*: Francesco Lavagnino and Alberto Barberis. *Music Conducted by*: Willy Ferrero. *Costumes*: Maria de Matteis. *Assistant Director*: Michael Washinsky. 91 minutes.

CAST. Orson Welles (*Othello*), Micheál MacLiammóir (*Iago*), Suzanne Cloutier (*Desdemona*), Robert Coote (*Roderigo*), Hilton Edwards (*Brabantio*), Michael Lawrence (*Cassio*), Fay Compton (*Emilia*), Nicholas Bruce (*Lodovico*), Jean Davis (*Montano*), Doris Dowling (*Bianca*).

Shot from 1949 to 1952, in the Scalera Studios, Rome, and in Morocco (Mogador, Safi, and Mazagan), and Italy (Venice, Tuscany, Rome, Viterbo, Perugia). Premiered at Cannes Film Festival in April 1952 (Grand Prix ex-aequo).

CONFIDENTIAL REPORT/MR. ARKADIN

Spain. 1955. A Mercury Production (Orson Welles). Filmorsa/Sevilla Studios. Released by Warner Bros. *Script*: Orson Welles, from his own novel, *Mr. Arkadin*. *Direction*: Orson Welles. *Photography*: Jean Bourgoin. *Editing*: Renzo Lucidi. *Production Design*: Orson Welles. *Music*: Paul Misraki. *Costumes*: Orson Welles. *Sound*: Jacques Lebreton and Jacques Carrère. *Script Girl*: Johanna Horward. *Assistant Directors*: José Mario Ochoa, De la Serna, Ferri. 99 minutes.

CAST. Orson Welles (*Gregory Arkadin*), Paola Mori (*Raina Arkadin*), Robert Arden (*Guy Van Stratten*), Michael Redgrave (*Burgomil Trebitsch*), Patricia Medina (*Mily*), Akim Tamiroff (*Jacob Zouk*), Mischa Auer (*The Professor*), Katina Paxinou (*Sophie*), Jack Watling (*Marquis of Rutleigh*), Grégoire Aslan (*Bracco*), Peter van Eyck (*Thaddeus*), Suzanne Flon (*Baroness Nagel*), O'Brady (*Oskar*), Tamara Shane (*The blonde*).

Shot in eight months during 1954, in France, Spain, Germany, and Italy. A Spanish version was also made, with Antonio Martinez in charge of editing, Amparo Rivelles as the Baroness Nagel, and Irene Lopez de Heredia as Sophie.

TOUCH OF EVIL

U.S.A. 1958. Produced and released by Universal International. *Script*: Orson Welles, from the novel *Badge of Evil,* by Whit Masterson. *Direction*: Orson Welles. *Photography*: Russell Metty. *Editing*: Virgil Vogel, Aaron Stell, Edward Curtiss. *Art Direction*: Alexander Golitzen and Robert Clatworthy. *Sets*: Russell A. Gausman and John Austin. *Music*: Henry Mancini. *Costumes*: Bill Thomas. *Sound*: Leslie I. Carey and Frank Wilkinson. *Camera Operator*: John Russell. *Assistant Directors*: Phil Bowles, Terry Nelson. *Producer*: Albert Zugsmith. 93 minutes.

CAST. Orson Welles (*Hank Quinlan*), Charlton Heston (*Ramon Miguel "Mike" Vargas*), Janet Leigh (*Susan Vargas*), Joseph Calleia (*Pete Menzies*), Akim Tamiroff (*"Uncle" Joe Grandi*), Joanna Moore (*Marcia*), Ray Collins (*District Attorney, Adair*), Dennis Weaver (*Night Porter*), Valentin De Vargas (*Pancho*), Mort Mills (*Schwartz*), Victor Millan (*Manelo Sanchez*), Lalo Rios (*Risto*), Michael Sargent (*Pretty boy*), Marlene Dietrich (*Tanya*), Joseph Cotten (*Coroner*), Zsa Zsa Gabor (*Striptease girl*), Mercedes McCambridge (*Girl in motel*), and Keenan Wynn.

Shot in 1957 in Universal Studios, Hollywood, and at Venice, California.

THE TRIAL
(Le Procès)

France/Italy/West Germany. 1962. Produced by Paris Europa Productions (Paris)/FI-C-IT (Rome)/Hisa-Films (Munich). *Script*: Orson Welles, from the novel by Franz Kafka. *Direction*: Orson Welles. *Photography*: Edmond Richard. *Editing*: Yvonne Martin. *Assistant Editors*: Chantal Delattre, Gérard Pollican. *Art Direction*: Jean Mandaroux. *Assistant Art Directors*: Jacques d'Ovidio, Jacques Brizzio, Pierre Tyberghien, Jean Bourlier. *Exterior Settings*: Guy Maugin. *Music*: Jean Ledrut, with the *Adagio* by Albinoni. *Special Effects Editor*: Denise Baby. *Pin-Screen Prologue*: Alexandre Alexeïeff and Claire Parker. *Cameraman*: Adolphe Charlet. *Assistant Camera Crew*: Max Dulac and Robert Fraisse. *Sound*: Guy Villette. *Assistant Sound Engineers*: Loiseau and Guy Maillet. *Sound Mixing*: Jacques Lebreton. *Make-up*: Louis Dor. *Wardrobe*: Hélène Thibault. *Continuity*: Marie-José Kling. *Production Manager*: Jacques Pignier. *Production Director*: Robert Florat. *Assistant Production Directors*: Marc Maurette and Paul Seban. *Stills*: Roger Corbeau. *Producers*: Alexander and Michael Salkind. 120 minutes.

CAST. Anthony Perkins (*Joseph K*), Orson Welles (*The Advocate, Hastler*), Jeanne Moreau (*Miss Burstner*), Romy Schneider (*Leni*), Elsa Martinelli (*Hilda*), Akim Tamiroff (*Block*), Arnoldo Foà (*Inspector*), William Kearns (*Assistant Inspector 1*), Jess Hahn (*Assistant Inspector 2*), Suzanne Flon (*Miss Pittl*), Madeleine Robinson (*Mrs. Grubach*), Wolfgang Reichmann (*Court room guard*), Thomas Holtzmann (*Law Student*), Maydra Shore (*Irmie*), Max Haufler (*Uncle Max*), William Chappell (*Titorelli*), Fernand Ledoux (*Chief Clerk*), Maurice Teynac (*Deputy Manager*), Michael Lonsdale (*The Priest*), Max Buchsbaum (*Examining Magistrate*), Raoul Delfosse (*First Executioner*), Jean-Claude Remoleux (*Second Executioner*), Karl Studer (*Man in Leather with Whip*), and Katina Paxinou and Van Doude (roles cut from final film).

Shot from March 26 to June 5, 1962, in the Studio de Boulogne, Paris, and in Zagreb, Globus, Dubrava, and Rome. Premiered December 21, 1962, in Paris.

CHIMES AT MIDNIGHT/FALSTAFF
(*Campanadas a medianoche*)

Spain/Switzerland. 1965/66. Internacional Films Española (Madrid) / Alpine (Basle). *Script*: Orson Welles, based on passages from *Richard II, Henry IV Pts I* and *II, Henry V,* and *The Merry Wives of Windsor,* by William Shakespeare. *Direction*: Orson Welles. *Photography*: Edmond Richard. *Editing*: Fritz Mueller. *Art Direction*: José Antonio de la Guerra, Mariano Erdoza. *Music*: Angelo Francesco Lavagnino. *Musical Direction*: Carlo Franci. *Costumes*: Orson Welles. *Sound Recording*: Peter Parasheles. *Commentary*: from Holinshed's *Chronicles.* *Narration*: Ralph Richardson. *Production Manager*: Gustavo Quintana. *Executive Producer*: Alessandro Tasca. *Producers*: Emiliano Piedra and Angel Escolano. *Assistant Director*: Tony Fuentes. 115 minutes (originally 119 minutes).

CAST. Orson Welles (*Sir John Falstaff*), Keith Baxter (*Prince Hal*), John Gielgud (*King Henry IV*), Jeanne Moreau (*Doll Tearsheet*), Margaret Rutherford (*Mistress Quickly*), Norman Rodway (*Henry "Hotspur" Percy*), Marina Vlady (*Kate Percy*), Alan Webb (*Justice Shallow*), Tony Beckley (*Poins*), Walter Chiari (*Silence*), Fernando Rey (*Worcester*), Michael Aldridge (*Pistol*), Beatrice Welles (*The Child*), Andrew Faulds (*Westmoreland*), José Nieto (*Northumberland*), with Paddy Bedford, Keith Pyott, Charles Farrell, Julio Peña, Fernando Hilbert, Andrés Mejuto.

Shot in the autumn and winter, 1965/66 on locations in Spain.

First screened at Cannes Film Festival, May 1966.

THE IMMORTAL STORY
(*Une Histoire immortelle*)

France. 1968. Albina Films/O.R.T.F. *Script*: Orson Welles, from the story by Isak Dinesen (pen name for Karen Blixen). *Direction*: Orson Welles. *Photography* (Eastmancolor): Willy Kurant. *Editing*: Yolande Maurette. *Assistant Editors*: Marcelle Pluet, Françoise Garnault, Claude Farney. *Art Direction*: André Piltant. *Music*: Erik Satie, played by Aldo Ciccolini and Jean-Noel Barbier. *Costumes*: Pierre Cardin (for Jeanne Moreau). *Sound Recording*: Jean Neny. *Production Manager*: Marc Morelle. *Assistant Directors*: Olivier Gérard, Tony Fuentes, Patrice Toron. *Producer*: Micheline Rozan. 60 minutes.

CAST. Orson Welles (*Mr. Clay*), Roger Coggio (*Elishama Levinsky*), Jeanne Moreau (*Virginie*), Norman Eshley (*Paul, the sailor*), Fernando Rey (*Man in street*).

Shot in Paris and Spain on behalf of French television in 1966. Televised and premiered theatrically in Paris on May 24, 1968.

DON QUIXOTE

Spain. 1955/71. An Oscar Dancigers Production. *Script*: Orson Welles, from the novel by Cervantes. *Direction*: Orson Welles. *Photography*: Jack Draper.

CAST. Orson Welles (*as himself*), Francisco Reiguera (*Don Quixote*), Akim Tamiroff (*Sancho Panza*), Patty McCormack (*Dulcinea*).

Shot in Mexico: Puebla, Tepozlan, Rio Frio; Paris; and Italy. Originally began as a thirty-minute TV show for Frank Sinatra.

THE DEEP

1967–? Shot in Yugoslavia under the title DEAD RECKONING, starring Welles, Laurence Harvey, and Jeanne Moreau.

THE OTHER SIDE OF THE WIND

1971– Some shooting already completed in Hollywood. Remainder probably in France.

Welles's Film Performances

1940 *Citizen Kane* (Charles Foster Kane). Directed by Welles.

1942 *Journey into Fear* (Colonel Haki). Directed by Norman Foster and also partly by Welles.

1943 *Jane Eyre* (Edward Rochester). Directed by Robert Stevenson.

1944 *Follow the Boys* (revue appearance with Marlene Dietrich). Directed by Eddie Sutherland.

1945 *Tomorrow Is Forever* (John Macdonald). Directed by Irving Pichel.

1946 *The Stranger* (Franz Kindler/Charles Rankin). Directed by Welles.

1947 *Black Magic* (Cagliostro). Directed by Gregory Ratoff.
The Lady from Shanghai (Michael O'Hara). Directed by Welles.

1948 *Macbeth* (Macbeth). Directed by Welles.
Prince of Foxes (Cesare Borgia). Directed by Henry King.

1949 *The Third Man* (Harry Lime). Directed by Carol Reed.

1950 *The Black Rose* (General Bayan). Directed by Henry Hathaway.

1951 *Return to Glennascaul* (Orson Welles). Directed by Hilton Edwards.
Othello (Othello). Directed by Welles.

Welles as Harry Lime enters the café near the end of THE THIRD MAN.

1953 *Trent's Last Case* (Sigsbee Manderson). Directed by Herbert Wilcox.

19 *Si Versailles m'était conté* (Benjamin Franklin). Directed by Sacha Guitry.

L'uomo, la bestia e la virtu (The Beast). Directed by Steno.

1954 *Napoléon* (Hudson Lowe). Directed by Sacha Guitry.

Three Cases of Murder (Lord Mountdrago). Directed by George More O'Ferrall (one episode only).

1955 *Confidential Report/Mr. Arkadin* (Gregory Arkadin). Directed by Welles.

Trouble in the Glen (Samin Cejador y Mengues). Directed by Herbert Wilcox.

1956 *Moby Dick* (Father Mapple). Directed by John Huston.

1957 *Pay the Devil* (Virgil Renckler). Directed by Jack Arnold.

The Long Hot Summer (Will Varner). Directed by Martin Ritt.

1958 *Touch of Evil* (Hank Quinlan). Directed by Welles.

The Roots of Heaven (Cy Sedgwick). Directed by John Huston.

Compulsion (Jonathan Wilk). Directed by Richard Fleischer.

1959 *David e Golia* (Saul). Directed by Richard Pottier/Ferdinando Baldi.

Ferry to Hong Kong (Captain Hart). Directed by Lewis Gilbert.

1960 *Austerlitz* (Fulton). Directed by Abel Gance.

Crack in the Mirror (Hagolin/Lamorcière). Directed by Richard Fleischer.

I Tartari (Burundai). Directed by Richard Thorpe.

1961 *Lafayette* (Benjamin Franklin). Directed by Jean Dréville.

Désordre. Short, directed by Jacques Baratier, in which Welles appeared briefly.

1962 *The Trial/Le Procès* (Hastler, the Advocate). Directed by Welles.

1963 *The V.I.P.s* (Max Buda). Directed by Anthony Asquith.

ROGOPAG (The Film Director). Directed by Pier Paolo Pasolini (one episode only).

1964 *La fabuleuse aventure de Marco Polo* (Ackermann). Directed by Denys de la Patellière and Noël Howard.

1965 *Chimes at Midnight/Falstaff/Campanadas a Medianoche* (Falstaff). Directed by Welles.

Casino Royale (Le Chiffre). Directed by John Huston *et al.*

Is Paris Burning?/Paris brûle-t-il? (Consul Raoul Nordling). Directed by René Clément.

Welles as Burundai in THE TARTARS.

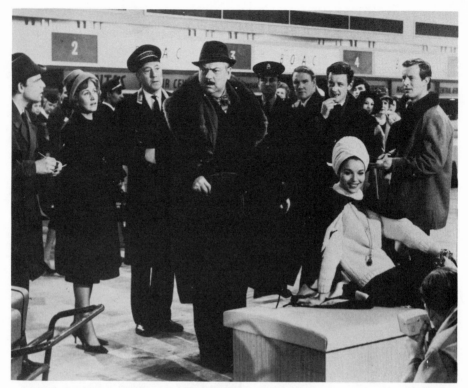

Welles as Max Buda in Anthony Asquith's THE V.I.P.s, with Elsa Martinelli in foreground.

1967   *The Sailor from Gibraltar* (Louis from Mozambique). Directed by Tony Richardson.

A Man for All Seasons (Cardinal Wolsey). Directed by Fred Zinnemann.

1968   *I'll Never Forget What's 'is Name* (Jonathan Lute). Directed by Michael Winner.

Oedipus the King (Tiresias). Directed by Philip Saville.

Une Histoire immortelle (Mr. Clay). Directed by Welles.

House of Cards (Charles Leschenhaut). Directed by John Guillermin.

Kampf um Rom (Emperor Justinian). Directed by Robert Siodmak.

1969   *The Southern Star* (Plankett). Directed by Sidney Hayers.

Tepepa/Viva la revolución (General Cascorro). Directed by Giulio Petroni.

12+1 (Markau). Directed by Nicolas Gessner.

Welles as Tiresias in OEDIPUS THE KING.

Curt Jürgens and Welles in the Yugoslavian spectacular, THE BATTLE OF NERETVA.

Battle of Neretva (Chetnik Senator). Directed by Veljko Bulajić.

1970   *Catch-22* (General Dreedle). Directed by Mike Nichols.
Waterloo (Louis XVIII). Directed by Sergei Bondarchuk.
The Kremlin Letter (Aleksei Bresnavitch). Directed by John Huston.
The Deep (Russ Brewer). Directed by Welles.

1971   *La Décade prodigieuse/Ten Days' Wonder* (Theo van Horn). Directed by Claude Chabrol.
Don Quixote (Orson Welles). Directed by Welles.
A Safe Place (The Magician). Directed by Henry Jaglom.
The Canterbury Tales (Old January). Directed by Pier Paolo Pasolini.

1972   *Sutjeska* (Winston Churchill). Directed by Stipe Delić.
Get to Know Your Rabbit. Directed by Brian De Palma.
Malpertuis. Directed by Harry Kümel.

Welles's Unrealised Film Projects

     * *denotes that scenario was actually written.*

* 1. *The Smiler with the Knife*. From the novel by Nicholas Blake. Planned in 1939.
* 2. *Heart of Darkness*. From the novel by Joseph Conrad. Planned in 1939.
* 3. *The Way to Santiago*. From the novel by Arthur Calder-Marshall. Planned in 1941.
* 4. *The Landru Story*. Written in 1944. This allegedly formed the basis for Chaplin's *Monsieur Verdoux*, though Chaplin recently disputed this.
* 5. *War and Peace*. From the novel by Leo Tolstoy. Planned in 1943.
* 6. *Crime and Punishment*. From the novel by Fyodor Dostoievsky. Planned in 1945.
* 7. *Henry IV*. From the play by Pirandello.
* 8. *Cyrano de Bergerac*. From the play by Edmond Rostand. Planned in 1947 with Alexander Korda.
* 9. *Moby Dick*. From the novel by Herman Melville.
*10. *Around the World in 80 Days*. Planned in 1948.
*11. *Ulysses*. A first scenario was written in 1949 by Ernest Borneman.
*12. *Julius Caesar*. From the play by William Shakespeare. In modern dress, planned for shooting in Rome in 1954.
*13. *Opération Cendrillon*.
*14. *Salome*.
*15. *Two by Two*. A modern version of Noah.

*16. *Paris by Night*. A film consisting of sketches. Planned with Alexander Korda.

*17. *Camille, the Naked Lady and the Musketeers*. A life of Alexandre Dumas.

18. *Le Portrait d'un Assassin*. Welles was to play a wall-of-death rider in a circus story.

19. *The Odyssey*, and/or *The Iliad*.

20. A screen version of Benvenuto Cellini's autobiography.

21. *Masquerade*.

22. *The Pickwick Papers*. From the novel by Charles Dickens.

23. *La Bibbia*. The Abraham episode for Dino de Laurentiis. "Abraham is my script. They shot it. I wrote it. They asked me to put my name on the credits but I refused. I was originally going to direct it. They used almost exactly the script I wrote . . ."[29]

24. *The Sacred Monsters*, a bull-fighting film set in Spain. "A different tone from Hemingway."

25. According to Charles Higham, Welles wrote the script of *Mexican Melodrama*, which was twice shelved in the early forties.

Films Narrated by Welles

1. *The Swiss Family Robinson* (directed by Edward Ludwig in 1940).

2. *The Magnificent Ambersons* and, according to Welles, "several hundred during the war period for American television."

3. *Duel in the Sun* (directed by King Vidor in 1946).

4. *Return to Glennascaul* (directed by Hilton Edwards in 1951).

5. *Les Seigneurs de la forêt/Lords of the Forest* (co-narrated by William Warfield. Directed by Heinz Sielman and Henry Brandt between 1956 and 1958).

6. *The Vikings* (directed by Richard Fleischer in 1958).

7. *High Journey* (directed by Peter Baylis in 1959).

8. *South Seas Adventure* (directed by Carl Dudley and others in 1959).

9. *King of Kings* (directed by Nicholas Ray in 1961).

10. *Der Grosse Atlantik/River of the Ocean* (directed by Peter Baylis in 1962).

11. *The Finest Hours* (directed by Peter Baylis in 1963).

12. *Around the World of Mike Todd* (directed for television by Saul Swimmer in 1968. Welles also appeared as he was speaking the commentary).

13. *Start the Revolution without Me* (directed by Bud Yorkin in 1969).

14. *Sentinels of Silence* (directed by Robert Amram in 1971).

15. *Directed by John Ford* (directed by Peter Bogdanovich in 1971).

16. *The Crucifixion* (directed by Robert Guenette in 1972).

Note: the above list is probably incomplete. To viewers of American television, Welles's voice, though often unidentified, is the familiar accompaniment to certain commercials.

Welles's Work in Television

1953   Played Lear in *King Lear* (directed by Peter Brook for C.B.S., New York).

1955   *The Orson Welles Sketchbook* (Six programmes, for B.B.C., London).

        Moby Dick (film of his stage version, made at the Hackney Empire and Scala Theatre. Never screened).

        Around the World with Orson Welles (13 half-hour programmes, not completed. For Associated Rediffusion, London).

1956   *Twentieth Century* (by Ben Hecht and Charles MacArthur. For C.B.S., New York).

1957   Abridged versions of *The Merchant of Venice, Macbeth,* and *Othello* (as actor. For C.B.S. and N.B.C., New York).

        Narrator for Archibald Macleish's *The Fall of the City.*

1958   *The Method* (A documentary on the Actors' Studio. For B.B.C., London). An incompleted film on Gina Lollobrigida.

        The Fountain of Youth. 30 minutes. Starring Dan Tobin, Joi Lansing, Rick Jason, and Billy House. (Pilot for ABC, screened on Colgate Half Hour.) See Joseph McBride[105] for a full description of this film.

1961   Film on the bullfight (as writer, director and narrator. For *Tempo,* ABC, London).

Note: Welles has made numerous appearances on talk shows in the U.S. and Britain, and has also narrated various TV films.

Welles's Work in Radio

1934   Acted as McGafferty in a condensed version of Archibald Macleish's *Panic.*

1934/35   Actor in *March of Time* series (for N.B.C.); also played several classical roles for N.B.C.

1936   Narrator of *Musical Reveries* (for C.B.S.); played Hamlet in *Hamlet,* directed for C.B.S. by Irving Reis.

1937   Played Lamont Cranston in *The Shadow,* a crime series for C.B.S.; adapted, directed, and played Jean Valjean in, *Les*

Misérables (for Mutual Broadcasting).

1938   *The Mercury Theatre on the Air:* series entitled "First Person Singular"—including adaptations of *Treasure Island, A Tale of Two Cities, The Thirty-Nine Steps, Abraham Lincoln* (Drinkwater), *Jane Eyre, The Man Who Was Thursday, Julius Caesar, Dracula,* and a programme of stories by Sherwood Anderson, Carl Ewald, and Saki.
"New Series": *Seventeen* (Booth Tarkington), *Around the World in 80 Days, Oliver Twist, The War of the Worlds* (for C.B.S.).

1941   *His Honor the Mayor* (play written, produced and narrated by Welles, for "The Free Company" on C.B.S.); also appeared on *The Lady Esther Show* (for C.B.S.).

1942/43   *Hello Americans* (weekly propaganda series. For C.B.S.); *The Orson Welles Show* (for C.B.S.).

1943   Series of political broadcasts (for A.B.C.); *Socony Vacuum* (series for C.B.S.); *This Is My Best* (series for C.B.S.).

1945   *The Mercury Theatre on the Air* (repeat, C.B.S.); series of talks on various subjects (for W.J.Z.).

1947   *The Mercury Theatre of the Air* (repeat C.B.S.); series of political broadcasts (for A.B.C.).

1951   *The Adventures of Harry Lime* (series of thirty-nine programmes, some written by Welles. Welles played Harry Lime. For B.B.C., London).

1952   *The Black Museum* (series of thirty-nine programmes on Scotland Yard cases, with Welles as actor and narrator. For B.B.C., London); *Sherlock Holmes* (with Welles as Moriarty. For B.B.C., London).

Welles's Stage Productions

1931   *The Lady from the Sea* (by Henrik Ibsen). Dublin Gate Theatre Studio.
The Three Sisters (by Anton Chekhov). Dublin Gate Theatre Studio.
Alice in Wonderland U.S.A. Dublin Gate Theatre Studio.

1934   *Trilby* (by Gerald du Maurier). Todd School, Woodstock.
The Drunkard (by Mr. Smith of Boston). Todd School, Woodstock.

1936   *Macbeth* (by William Shakespeare). Federal Theatre at Lafayette Th., Harlem, N.Y.
Horse Eats Hat (adapted by Welles from Labiche's "Un

Chapeau de paille d'Italie"). Federal Theatre at Maxine Elliott Th., N.Y.

1937 *Doctor Faustus* (by Christopher Marlowe). Federal Theatre at Maxine Elliott Th., N.Y.

The Cradle Will Rock (by Marc Blitztein). Federal Theatre at Venice Th., N.Y.

Julius Caesar (by William Shakespeare). Mercury Theatre at Comedy Th., N.Y. Later at National Th., N.Y.

1938 *The Shoemaker's Holiday* (by Thomas Dekker). Mercury Theatre at Comedy Th., N.Y.

Heartbreak House (by Bernard Shaw). Mercury Theatre at Comedy Th., N.Y.

Too Much Johnson (by William Gillette, adapted by Welles). Stony Creek Summer Theatre.

Danton's Death (by Georg Büchner). Mercury Theatre at Comedy Th., N.Y.

1939 *The Five Kings* (adapted by Welles from *Henry IV, Pts. I & II; Henry V; Henry VI, Pts. I-III; Richard II;* and *Richard III* by William Shakespeare). Theatre Guild at Boston, Colonial Th.

The Green Goddess (by William Archer, adapted by Welles). R.K.O. Vaudeville Circuit.

The Second Hurricane (opera by Aaron Copland).

1941 *Native Son* (by Paul Green, Richard Wright). St. James Theatre, N.Y.

1942 *Mercury Wonder Show.* Performances for the troops on Cahuenga Boulevard, Los Angeles.

1946 *Around the World* (by Welles, Cole Porter). Adelphi Theatre, N.Y.

1947 *Macbeth* (by William Shakespeare). Utah Centennial Festival, Salt Lake City.

1950 *Time Runs* (by Welles). Théâtre Edouard VII, Paris.

The Unthinking Lobster (by Welles). Théâtre Edouard VII, Paris.

1951 *Othello* (by William Shakespeare). St. James's Theatre, London.

1955 *Moby Dick* (by Welles). Duke of York's Theatre, London.

1956 *King Lear* (by William Shakespeare). City Center, New York.

1960 *Rhinoceros* (by Eugène Ionesco). Royal Court Theatre, London.

Welles's Stage Performances

1931 Duke Alexander of Wurtemberg in *The Jew Süss* (by Leon

Feuchtwanger) , at Dublin Gate Theatre.

Ralph Bentley in *The Dead Ride Fast* (by David Sears) at Dublin Gate Theatre.

General Bazaine in *The Archduke* (by Percy Robinson) at Dublin Gate Theatre.

The Grand Vizier in *Mogu of the Desert* (by Padraic O'Conaire) at Dublin Gate Theatre.

1932   Duke Lamberto in *Death Takes a Holiday* (by Alberto Casella) at Dublin Gate Theatre.

The Ghost and Fortinbras in *Hamlet* (by William Shakespeare) at Dublin Gate Theatre.

Lord Porteus in *The Circle* (by W. Somerset Maugham) at the Abbey Theatre, Dublin.

Note: Welles played minor parts in several plays at the Gate and Abbey Theatres during his stay in Dublin. These included: *King John, Richard III, Timon of Athens* (Shakespeare) ; *The Emperor Jones* (O'Neill) ; *The Father* (Strindberg) ; *The Devil; Grumpy* (Hodges and Percival) ; *Peer Gynt* (Ibsen) ; *Mr. Wu* (Vernon and Owen) ; *Dr. Knock* (Romains) ; *La Locandiera* (Goldoni) ; *The Rivals* (Sheridan) ; *The Play's the Thing* (Molnar) ; *Volpone* (Ben Johnson) ; *Man and Superman* (Bernard Shaw) ; *The Makropoulos Secret* (Capek) ; and *The Dover Road* (A. A. Milne) .

1933   Octavius Barrett in *The Barretts of Wimpole Street* (by Rudolph Besier) with the Katharine Cornell Company on tour. Marchbanks in *Candida* (by Bernard Shaw) with the Katharine Cornell Company on tour.

1934   Mercutio in *Romeo and Juliet* (by William Shakespeare) with the Katharine Cornell Company on tour.

Svengali in *Trilby* (by George du Maurier) at the Todd school, Woodstock.

Claudius in *Hamlet* (by William Shakespeare) at the Todd School, Woodstock.

Count Pahlen in *Czar Paul* (by Merejowski) at the Todd School, Woodstock.

Chorus and Tybalt in *Romeo and Juliet* (by William Shakespeare) with the Katharine Cornell Company at Martin Beck Th., New York.

1935   McGafferty in *Panic* (by Archibald Macleish) , with the Phoenix Theatre Group at Imperial Th., N.Y.

1936   André Pequot in *Ten Million Ghosts* (by Sidney Kingsley) at St. James Theatre, New York.

1937   Faustus in *Doctor Faustus* (by Christopher Marlowe) with the Federal Theatre at Maxine Elliott Th., N.Y.

Brutus in *Julius Caesar* (by William Shakespeare) with the Mercury Theatre at Century Th., New York.

1938   Captain Shotover in *Heartbreak House* (by Bernard Shaw) with the Mercury Theatre at Comedy Th., N.Y.

Saint-Just in *Danton's Death* (by Georg Büchner) with the Mercury Theatre at Comedy Th., N.Y.

1939   Falstaff and Richard III in *The Five Kings* (adapted by Welles from plays by Shakespeare) with the Theatre Guild at Colonial Theatre, Boston.

The Rajah in *The Green Goddess* (by William Archer, adapted by Welles) on the R.K.O. Vaudeville Circuit.

1942   A Magician act in *The Mercury Wonder Show*, on Cahuenga Boulevard, Los Angeles.

1946   Dick Fix, the Detective in *Around the World* (by Welles, Cole Porter) at the Adelphi Theatre, New York.

1947   Macbeth in *Macbeth* (by William Shakespeare) at the Utah Centennial Festival, Salt Lake City.

1950   Doctor Faustus in *Time Runs* (by Welles) at Théâtre Edouard VII, Paris.

Jake in *The Unthinking Lobster* (by Welles) at Théâtre Edouard VII, Paris.

1951   Othello in *Othello* (by William Shakespeare) at St. James's Theatre, London.

1955   The Actor Manager, Captain Ahab, and Father Mapple in *Moby Dick* (by Welles) at Duke of York's Theatre, London.

1956   Lear in *King Lear* (by William Shakespeare) at the City Center, New York.

1960   Falstaff in *Chimes at Midnight* (adapted from William Shakespeare) at the Grand Opera House, Belfast.

APPENDIX 5

Bibliography

Note: the reference numbers quoted in the text of the book refer to the books and articles below.

A. BOOKS BY WELLES

1. "Everybody's Shakespeare" (1933, with illustrations by Welles), and a subsequent revision of this entitled "The Mercury Shakespeare" (1939).
2. "Une Grosse Légume," translated by Maurice Bessy (Gallimard, Paris, 1953). A satirical novel.
3. "A Bon Entendeur," translated by Serge Greffet (Editions de la Table Ronde, Paris, 1953). Includes Welles's two-act play *Fair Warning*.
4. "Mr. Arkadin" (W. H. Allen, London, 1956). Novel on which Welles's film *Confidential Report/Mr. Arkadin* was based. First published in French in 1954 by Gallimard, Paris.

B. PUBLISHED SCRIPTS BY WELLES

5. *Citizen Kane* (complete, with details of camera movements and positions, and of the soundtrack). Number 11 in the series *L'Avant-Scène du Cinéma*, Paris, January 1962. In French. Now also available in English (shooting script plus a continuity) in "The *Citizen Kane* Book" (Little, Brown, Boston; Secker and Warburg, London, 1971).
6. *The Trial/Le Procès* (complete, with details of camera movements and positions, and of the soundtrack). Number 23 in the series *L'Avant-Scène du Cinéma*, Paris, February 1963. In French. Now also available in English (Lorrimer Publications, London; Simon and Schuster, New York, 1970).

7. *The Magnificent Ambersons.* Short extracts first published in *La Revue du Cinéma,* Number 3, Paris, December 1946, and reprinted in *Premier Plan,* Lyon, Number 16, March 1961. In French.
8. Scripts of *Confidential Report/Mr. Arkadin, Touch of Evil,* and *The Trial,* in Spanish (*Temas de Cine,* Madrid, 1962).

C. ARTICLES BY WELLES

9. "Je combats comme un géant dans un monde de nains pour le cinéma universel," in *Arts,* Paris, August 25, 1954.
10. "Un ruban de rêves," in *L'Express,* Paris, June 5, 1958, and reprinted in English in *International Film Annual,* Number 2 (John Calder, London, 1958).
11. "The Scenario Crisis," in *International Film Annual,* Number 1 (John Calder, London, 1957).
12. Letter to the *New Statesman,* London, May 24, 1958, concerning *Touch of Evil.*
13. Letter to *The Times,* London, November 17, 1971, concerning the script of *Citizen Kane.*
14. Preface to *Put Money in Thy Purse,* by Micheál MacLiammóir (Methuen, London, 1952).
15. Preface to *Les Truquages au Cinéma,* by Maurice Bessy (Editions Prisma, Paris, 1951).
16. Preface to *Précis de Prestidigitation,* by Bruce Elliott (Editions Payot, Switzerland).
17. "The Third Audience," in *Sight and Sound,* London, January-March 1954.
18. Series of articles in *Free Worlds, The New York Post,* and *The Farmer Almanac* (1942–45).
19. Preface to *He That Plays the King,* by Kenneth Tynan (Longmans, London, 1950).
20. Series of reflections in *La Démocratie Combattante,* Paris, April-May 1952.
21. "But Where Are We Going?" in *Look,* New York, November 3, 1970.

D. INTERVIEWS WITH WELLES

22. Bazin, André, and Tacchella, Jean-Charles. Interview in *L'Ecran Français,* Number 169, Paris, September 21, 1948.
23. Bazin, André, and Bitsch, Charles. "Entretien avec Orson

Welles," in *Cahiers du Cinéma*, Paris, Number 84, June, 1958.

24. Bazin, André. "Orson Welles, la télévision et le magnétophone," in *France-Observateur*, Paris, June 12, 1958.

25. Bazin, André, Bitsch, Charles, and Domarchi, Jean. "Nouvel Entretien avec Orson Welles," in *Cahiers du Cinéma*, Paris, Number 87, September 1958.

26. Bucher, Felix, and Cowie, Peter. "Welles and Chabrol," in *Sight and Sound*, London, Autumn 1971. Other parts of this interview, not published in *Sight and Sound*, are quoted in the present book.

27. Clay, Jean. Interview in *Réalités*, Number 201, Paris, 1962.

28. Cobos, Juan, and Rubio, Miguel. "Welles and Falstaff," in *Sight and Sound*, Autumn 1966. London.

29. Cobos, Juan, Rubio, Miguel, and Pruneda, Jose Antonio. "Voyage au pays de Don Quixote," in *Cahiers du Cinéma*, Paris, Number 165, April 1965. Reprinted (translated by Rose Kaplin) in *Cahiers du Cinéma in English*, New York, Number 5, 1966, and in *Interviews with Film Directors*, edited by Andrew Sarris (Bobbs Merrill, New York, 1967) and *Hollywood Voices* (Secker and Warburg, London, 1971).

30. Grigs, Derrick. "Conversation at Oxford," in *Sight and Sound*, London, Spring 1960.

31. Halton, Kathleen. Interview on BBC programme *The Movies*, 1967.

32. Koval, Francis. "Interview with Welles," in *Sight and Sound*, London, December 1950. Reprinted in *Film Makers on Film Making*, edited by Harry M. Geduld (University of Indiana Press, Bloomington, 1967).

33. Magnan, Henry. "Orson Welles s'explique," in *Les Lettres Françaises*, Number 727, Paris, June 19, 1958.

34. Powell, Dilys. "The Life and Opinions of Orson Welles," in *The Sunday Times*, London, February 3, 1963.

35. Silverman, Doré. "Odd Orson," in *You*, London, July-August 1951.

36. Tynan, Kenneth. "Playboy Interview: Orson Welles," in *Playboy*, Chicago, March 1967.

37. "Une Conférence de presse," (Brussels Festival, June 8, 1958), in *Cahiers du Cinéma*, Number 87, Paris, September 1958.

38. Interview in *Variety*, New York, January 5, 1966.

39. Interview in Atticus column, *The Sunday Times*, London, February 26, 1967.

E. BOOKS AND MONOGRAPHS ON WELLES

40. Allais, Jean-Claude. "Orson Welles," in *Premier Plan,* Number 16, 1961 (SERDOC, Lyon), in French.

41. Bazin, André. "Orson Welles," with a Preface by Jean Cocteau (Editions Chavane, Paris, 1950).

42. Bessy, Maurice. "Orson Welles," *Cinéma d'Aujourd'hui* Series, Number 6 (Editions Seghers, Paris 1963 and 1970). Includes much writing by Welles himself, and extracts from the scripts of *Citizen Kane, The Magnificent Ambersons, The Trial,* and *Salome* (never filmed). Revised edition translated into English and published in 1971 by Crown, New York.

43. Bogdanovich, Peter. "The Cinema of Orson Welles" (Film Library of the Museum of Modern Art, New York, 1961).

44. Bogdanovich, Peter, and Welles, Orson. "This Is Orson Welles" (New York, 1972?).

45. Cowie, Peter. "El Cine de Orson Welles" (Ediciones Era, Mexico City, 1969). Spanish version of original paperback on which present book is based.

46. Fowler, Roy Alexander. "Orson Welles, A First Biography" (Pendulum Publications, London, 1946).

47. Higham, Charles. "The Films of Orson Welles" (University of California Press, Berkeley and London, 1970/71).

48. Kael, Pauline. "The *Citizen Kane* Book" (Little, Brown, Boston; Secker and Warburg, London, 1971). Contains essay, "Raising Kane," first published in *The New Yorker,* New York, 1971.

49. MacLiammóir, Micheál. "Put Money in Thy Purse," with a Preface by Orson Welles (Methuen, London, 1952). A brilliantly written diary of the filming of *Othello.*

50. McBride, Joseph. "Orson Welles" (Secker and Warburg, London, 1972).

51. Noble, Peter. "The Fabulous Orson Welles" (Hutchinson, London, 1956).

52. "Orson Welles, l'éthique et l'esthétique," by various authors (Etudes Cinématographiques, Numbers 24/25, Paris, 1963).

F. GENERAL

53. Agel, Henri. "Les Grands Cinéastes" (Editions Universitaires, Paris, 1959).

54. ———. "Romance Américaine" (Editions du Cerf, Paris, 1963). Includes a chapter on *Touch of Evil.*

55. Andreas, Cyrus. "I'm a Lurid Character!" A Note on Orson Welles, in *Film Miscellany*, Winter 1946/47.

56. Bazin, André. "L'Apport d'Orson Welles," in *Ciné-Club*, Number 7, May 1948.

57. ———. "Orson Welles chez les Jivaros," in *Cahiers du Cinéma*, Number 88, Paris, October 1958.

58. Bentley, Eric. "*Othello* on Film," in *New Republic*, New York, October 3, 1955.

59. Béranger, Jean. "Citizen Welles," in *Kosmorama*, Copenhagen, October and December 1962.

60. Bessy, Maurice. "Les vertes statues d'Orson Welles," in *Cahiers du Cinéma*, Paris, May 1952.

61. Billard, Pierre. "*Chimes at Midnight*," in *Sight and Sound*, London, Spring 1965.

62. Bitsch, Charles. "Orson Welles consacré Shakespeare au Cinéma au Festival mondial du film à Bruxelles," in *Arts*, Paris, June 18, 1958.

63. Björkman, Stig. "My Name Is Orson Welles," in *Chaplin*, Stockholm, Number 33, 1962.

64. Borde, Raymond, and Chaumeton, Etienne. "Panorama du film noir Américain" (Editions de Minuit, Paris, 1955). A particularly good section on *The Lady from Shanghai*.

65. Bordwell, David. "*Citizen Kane*," in *Film Comment*, New York, Summer 1971.

66. Bourgeois, Jacques. "Le Cinéma à la recherche du temps perdu," in *La Revue du Cinéma*, Paris, December 1946.

67. ———, and Doniol-Valcroze, Jacques. "Orson Welles enchaîné," in *La Revue du Cinéma*, Paris, Autumn, 1947. On *Journey into Fear* and *The Stranger*.

68. ———. "Le Sujet et l'expression au cinéma," in *La Revue du Cinéma*, Paris, October 1948. On *Macbeth*.

69. Capdenac, Michel. "Citizen K," in *Les Lettres Françaises*, Paris, December 27, 1962. On *The Trial*.

70. Castello, G. C. "The Magnificent Orson W," in *Bianco e nero*, Rome, January 1949.

71. Cau, Jean. "Trois Jours avec Orson Welles," in *L'Express*, Paris, 19?

72. Chappell, William. "Orson Welles Films Kafka," in *The Sunday Times*, London, May 27, 1962.

73. Chartier, Jean-Pierre. "Les Films 'à la première personne' et l'illusion de la réalité au cinéma," in *La Revue du Cinéma*, Paris, January 1947.

74. Chaumeton, Etienne. "Notes récentes sur *La Splendeur des Amberson*," in *Cinéma 56*, Paris, Number 7, 1956.

75. Cocteau, Jean. Profile of Welles, in *Cinémonde*, Paris, March 6, 1950.

76. Coursodon, J-P. *"Citizen Kane,"* in *Cinéma 60*, Paris, Number 43, 1960.

77. Cowie, Peter. "Orson Welles," in *Films and Filming*, London, April 1961.

78. Cutts, John. *"Citizen Kane,"* in *Films and Filming*, December 1963.

79. Domarchi, Jean. "Welles a n'en plus finir," in *Cahiers du Cinéma*, Number 85, Paris, July 1958.

80. ———. "America," in *Cahiers du Cinéma*, Paris, November 1959. On *Citizen Kane*.

81. Doniol-Valcroze, Jacques. "Le Triomphe d'une bonne intention," in *La Revue du Cinéma*, Paris, December 1946. On *Citizen Kane*.

82. ———. "Rita est morte, à l'aube, seule . . . ," in *La Revue du Cinéma*, Paris, March 1948. On *The Lady from Shanghai*.

83. Dorigo, Francesco. "Orson Welles tra Kafka e Dostoivskij," in *Cine Forum*, Venice, December 1963.

84. Dorsday, Michel. "Othello ou la solitude de notre temps," in *Cahiers du Cinéma*, Paris, October 1952.

85. Egly, Max. "Retour de Welles," in *Image et Son*, Number 139, Paris, March 1961.

86. Gerasimov, Sergei. "All Is Not Welles," in *Films and Filming*, London, September 1959.

87. Giametteo, Feraldo di. *"Macbeth,"* in *Bianco e nero*, Rome, July 1948.

88. Gilliatt, Penelope. Review of *The Trial*, in *The Observer*, London, November 17, 1963.

89. Gottesman, Ronald (editor). "Focus on *Citizen Kane*" (Prentice Hall, Englewood Cliffs, New Jersey, 1971).

90. Haulotte, Edgar. "La Logique d'*Othello*," in *Positif*, Paris, Number 6.

91. Jacob, Gilles. "Le Cinéma Moderne" (SERDOC, Lyon, 1964). Especially good on *The Lady from Shanghai* and *Touch of Evil*.

92. Johnson, William. "Orson Welles: Of Time and Loss," in *Film Quarterly*, Berkeley, Fall 1967.

93. Kafka, Franz. "The Trial," with an Introduction by Max Brod, translated by Willa and Edwin Muir (Secker and Warburg/ Penguin Books, London).

94. Kerr, Walter. "Wonder Boy Welles," in *Theatre Arts,* New York, September 1951.

95. Labarthe, André S. "My Name is Orson Welles," in *Cahiers du Cinéma,* Number 117, Paris, March 1961.

96. Lebel, Jean-Patrick. *"Le Procès,"* in *Contrechamp,* Marseille, April 1963.

97. Leenhardt, Roger. *"Citizen Kane,"* in *L'Ecran Français,* Paris, July 3, 1946.

98. Leigh, Janet (in conversation with Rui Noguiera). "Psycho, Rosie and a Touch of Orson," in *Sight and Sound,* London, Spring 1970.

99. Leonard, Harold. "Notes on *Macbeth,"* in *Sight and Sound,* London, March 1950.

100. Lightman, Herb A. *"The Lady from Shanghai,* Field Day for the Camera," in *The American Cinematographer,* Los Angeles, June 1947.

101. MacLiammóir, Micheál. "Orson Welles," in *Sight and Sound,* London, July–September 1954.

102. Manuel, Jacques. "Essai sur le style d'Orson Welles," in *La Revue du Cinéma,* Paris, December 1946.

103. Marcorelles, Louis. *"La Soif du mal,"* in *Cinéma 58,* Number 29, Paris, 1958.

104. Martinez, Enrique. "The Trial of Orson Welles," in *Films and Filming,* London, October 1962.

105. McBride, Joseph. "First Person Singular," in *Sight and Sound,* London, Winter 1971/72. On Welles's TV film, *The Fountain of Youth.*

106. ———. *"Citizen Kane,"* in *Film Heritage,* Fall 1968.

107. ———. *"The Magnificent Ambersons,"* in "Persistence of Vision" (Wisconsin Film Society Press, Madison, 1968).

108. ———. "Welles before *Kane,"* in *Film Quarterly,* Berkeley, Spring 1970.

109. ———. "Welles' *Immortal Story,"* in *Sight and Sound,* London, Autumn 1970.

110. ———. Reasoned attack on the Pauline Kael *Kane* arguments, in *Film Heritage,* Fall 1971.

111. Miller, Claude. Fiche on *The Trial,* in *Téléciné,* Paris, Number 110, April–May 1963.

112. Nowák, Petr. "Kafka's Prague," in *The Observer,* London, November 17, 1963.

113. O'Brady, Frédéric. "Le Troisième Homme et le deuxième Arkadin," in *Cahiers du Cinéma,* Paris, July 1956.

114. Pariante, Roberto. "Orson Welles from *Citizen Kane* to *Othello*," in *Bianco e nero*, Rome, March 1956.

115. Pechter, William S. "Trials," in *Sight and Sound*, London, Winter 1963/64.

116. Prokosch, Mike. "Orson Welles," in *Film Comment*, New York, Summer 1971.

117. Raynor, Henry. "Shakespeare Filmed," in *Sight and Sound*, London, July–September 1952.

118. Robson, Mark, quoted in "The Celluloid Muse," (edited by Higham and Greenberg) (Angus and Robertson, London, 1969).

119. Rohmer, Eric. "Une Fable du XXe siècle," in *Cahiers du Cinéma*, Paris, July 1956. On *Confidential Report/Mr. Arkadin*.

120. Sadoul, Georges. "Histoire du Cinéma Mondial" (Flammarion, Paris 1961—revised edition).

121. Sarris, Andrew. "*Citizen Kane:* the American Baroque," in *Film Culture*, New York, Volume 2, Number 3, 1956.

122. Sartre, Jean-Paul. "Quand Hollywood veut faire penser," and "*Citizen Kane*," in *L'Ecran Français*, Paris, August 1, 1945.

123. Shivas, Mark. "*The Trial,*" in *Movie*, London, February–March 1963.

124. Siclier, Jacques. "Le Mythe de la femme dans le cinéma Américain" (Editions du Cerf, Paris, 1956). Parts devoted to *Citizen Kane* and, in particular, to *The Lady from Shanghai*.

125. Silver, Charles. "*The Immortal Story,*" in *Film Comment*, New York, Summer 1971.

126. Sloane, Everett. An interview in *Film*, London, Number 37, 1963.

127. Soriano, Marc. "Cinq remarques sur Orson Welles à propos de *La Splendeur des Amberson*," in *La Revue du Cinéma*, Paris, February 1947.

128. Stanbrook, Alan. "The Heroes of Welles," in *Film*, London, Number 28, 1961.

129. Stein, Elliott. Article on *The Trial*, in *The Financial Times*, London, February 18, 1963.

130. Toland, Gregg. "How I Broke the Rules in *Citizen Kane*," in *Popular Photoplay Magazine*, Number 8, June 1941.

131. ———. Article on *Kane*'s camerawork in *The American Cinematographer*, Los Angeles, February 1941.

132. ———. "L'Opérateur de prises de vues," in *La Revue du Cinéma*, Paris, January 1947.

133. Truffaut, François. *"Citizen Kane,"* in *L'Express,* Paris, November 26, 1959.

134. Tynan, Kenneth. "Orson Welles," in *Show,* October and November 1961.

135. Viazzi, Glauco. *"Citizen Kane,"* in *Bianco e nero,* Rome, July 1948.

136. Weinberg, Herman G. *"Confidential Report/Mr. Arkadin,"* in *Film Culture,* New York, Volume 2, Number 3, 1956.

137. ———. *"Touch of Evil,"* in *Film Culture,* New York, Number 20, 1959.

138. ———. "The Legion of Lost Films," in *Sight and Sound,* London, Autumn 1962.

139. Wilson, Richard. "It's Not *Quite* All True," in *Sight and Sound,* London, Autumn 1970. A critical comment on Charles Higham's version of Welles's adventures with *It's All True* (see item 47).

140. "L'Oeuvre d'Orson Welles," in *Cahiers du Cinéma,* Paris, Number 87, September 1958. Useful biofilmography up to 1958, illustrated with rare photographs.

141. Entire issue of *Cine Forum,* Venice, Number 19, 1962, devoted to Welles.

142. Section: "Le Procès d'Orson Welles," in *Cinéma 62,* Paris, Number 71, 1962.

143. "Orson Welles, sa vie et ses oeuvres," biofilmography in *Cinéma 62,* Paris, Number 71, 1962.

144. "A Saint for the Cinema," in *Contemporary Dancers' Centre,* November 1960.

145. Reprint of the 1938 broadcast version of H. G. Wells's "The War of the Worlds," in *Film Culture,* New York, Number 27, 1962/63.

146. "Welles contra Hitchcock," in *Film Forum,* Voorhout (Holland), Number 3, 1959.

147. Entire issue of *Image et Son,* Paris, Number 139, 1961, devoted to Welles.

148. "Hommage à Orson Welles," by Louis Aragon, Alexandre Astruc, Edmonde Charles-Roux, Jean Cocteau, Roger Leenhardt, Jean Dutourd, Joseph Kessel, Philippe Soupault and Louise de Vilmorin in *Les Lettres Françaises,* Paris, November 26, 1959.

149. "Checklist 10—Orson Welles," in *Monthly Film Bulletin,* London, January and February 1964.

150. "Winged Gorilla," in *New Statesman and Nation,* London, January 21, 1956. A general article on Welles and his work, anonymous.

151. "Orson Welles," in *The Observer,* London, November 20, 1955. A profile.

152. "Débat sur *Le Procès,*" in *Positif,* Paris, Numbers 50–52, March 1963.

INDEX